Agenda for the 90s

Forging the Future of Adult Religious Education

Neil A. Parent
General Editor

Department of Education
United States Catholic Conference

In its 1987 planning document, as approved by the general membership of the United States Catholic Conference in November 1986, the Department of Education was authorized to continue with the publication of an annual resource book for adult religious education. This current publication, *Agenda for the 90s: Forging the Future of Adult Religious Education*, has been prepared by Mr. Neil A. Parent, Coordinator for the Division of Catechesis/Faith Formation, approved by Rev. Thomas G. Gallagher, Secretary of Education, and authorized for publication by the undersigned.

Monsignor Daniel F. Hoye
General Secretary
August 19, 1988   NCCB/USCC

Typeface: Palatino
Typography: World Composition Services, Inc.
            Sterling, Virginia

ISBN 1-55586-243-8

Contents

Introduction / 1
Neil A. Parent

I. The Mature Christian Adult / 3
    Loretta Girzaitis

    Reclaiming Meaning: A Response to
    The Mature Christian Adult / 13
    Fred Eyerman

II. Leadership in Adult Religious Education / 19
     David M. Thomas

     Leader as Manager? A Response to Leadership
     in Adult Religious Education / 26
     Jane Wolford Hughes

III. Theological Perspectives on Adult Religious Education / 33
      John L. Elias

      A Church That Learns: A Response to Theological
      Perspectives on Adult Religious Education / 41
      John R. Zaums

IV. Unity and Diversity within Adult Religious Education / 45
     C. Michael Lebrato

     Reflections While Working Out at the YMCA: A Response to
     Unity and Diversity within Adult Religious Education / 53
     Alice M. Stefaniak

V. The Social and Cultural Context of Adult Religious
    Education / 57
    Maurice L. Monette, OMI

    The Challenge to Be Relevant and Effective: A Response
    to The Social and Cultural Content of Adult Religious
    Education / 65
    Matthew Hayes

VI. About the Authors / 71

Introduction

In the mid-1970s, a group of mostly diocesan adult educators were invited by the Department of Education, United States Catholic Conference, to identify some of the key issues facing adult religious education. After an extensive consultation process, the department published in 1977 the *Critical Issues* report. Essentially, the report identified five issues that represented the "patterns, trends, and possibilities for the future of adult religious education" and presented action steps for addressing each of them. The action steps were updated in 1979.

In the years that followed, many, if not most, of the major developments in adult education stemming from the United States Catholic Conference grew from seeds planted in the *Critical Issues* project. For example, the publications, *Ministering to Adult Learners*, the five volumes of *Christian Adulthood*, and the major adult religious education resource paper, *Serving Life and Faith*, came either directly or indirectly from the *Critical Issues* action plans. Also, the National Project on Adult Learning and the Parish was an outgrowth of the *Critical Issues* project.

In 1980, the group of diocesan adult educators who had worked on the *Critical Issues* Project was organized by the USCC into the National Advisory Committee on Adult Religious Education (NACARE). Since then, NACARE has been actively providing leadership for the Department of Education on a wide range of adult education issues and projects.

About two years ago, NACARE began to develop what it termed *The Agenda for the 90s* to serve adult religious education in the last decade of this century the way *Critical Issues* had done in the late 70s and early 80s. This book represents a major step in that planning process by presenting five important issues that NACARE sees itself needing to address in the remaining years of this century.

The five issues that NACARE has identified are: (1) supporting the process of Christian maturation through learning, (2) developing competent leadership in adult religious education, (3) articulating a theological vision of adult religious education, (4) achieving unity within diversity in the practice of adult religious education, (5) and understanding and using the social context in planning for adult religious education. Each of these issues is addressed by a noted adult religious educator, and a response article draws out the practical implications.

Although each of the primary authors wrote his or her article from guidelines that were developed by NACARE, these authors are basically presenting their own views on the issues and not those of NACARE or of the USCC Department of Education, USCC.

1

It is NACARE's hope that *Agenda for the 90s: Forging the Future of Adult Religious Education* will stimulate wide-ranging discussion and continuing refinement of these issues. Indeed, between now and 1990, NACARE intends to further develop each of the issues and to identify appropriate action steps for addressing them.

Just as NACARE was a development from the ad hoc group of diocesan adult educators convened by the USCC, so this book is a development from the *Christian Adulthood* series. After the fifth volume of *Christian Adulthood* was published, we felt that a different kind of resource might be more appropriate for serving the needs of today's adult education practitioner. Rather than to continue to publish a collection of articles on various topics of adult religious education, we decided to focus on one key theme for each volume and to use a title for the book that reflects the theme. But, although the new publication's format and title are different, we continue with the spirit and tradition of *Christian Adulthood*.

Neil A. Parent
General Editor
Division of Catechesis/Faith Formation
Department of Education
United States Catholic Conference

2

The Mature Christian Adult

Loretta Girzaitis

"Who am I?" is a perennial question that surfaces in an individual's lifetime. A person asks it in childhood, struggles with it in adolescence, focuses on it in early childhood, is challenged by it in midlife, and may, finally, come to terms with it in old age.

As one encounters life, experiences suggest responses to that question, while, at the same time, they raise other substantive questions: "Why am I here?" "Where am I going?" "How will I get there?" The underlying factor beyond the questioning is a restless and continuous search for meaning.

"What's it all about?" was Alfie's cry. That same cry is repeated by others also, whether these be parents, business executives, sports heroes, or other public figures searching for their identity as persons. It is echoed by those in the trauma of illness, unemployment, or failure. It is sounded by those experiencing adulation and favor. It is persistent in both the lowly and the arrogant, the joyful and the troubled, the successful and the unfortunate. It may or may not be articulated but, as a parasite, it persists within a person's unconscious throughout a lifetime.

This search for value, for meaning in one's life, is the ongoing process of maturation, and neither age nor status complete it or bring it to fruition. The essence of Self is discovered, developed, and embraced only through constant and lifelong consciousness and effort. It is through daily challenges, demands, and decisions that individuals move along to make sense of their daily lives. Even at the end of life, one may be unsure and unclear of the result since the feeling of incompleteness may persist.

So, the achievement of maturity is an ideal and not something that is accomplished with finality somewhere in life. Therefore, there is a need to be open to the Spirit who calls, cajoles, comforts, and creates new yearnings and new visions. But when a person responds and participates, movement is virtually guaranteed.

The search for meaning takes on Christian dimensions when it acknowledges that God intends wholeness for each individual. Paul emphasizes this process in his letter to the Ephesians: " . . . you should put away the old self of your former way of life, corrupted through deceitful desires, and be renewed in the spirit of your minds, and put on the new self, created in God's way in righteousness and holiness of truth" (Ephesians 4:22-24).

Today's adults face a variety of issues, developments, and experiences that, because of their unpredictableness, disturb the simplistic worldview which many possess. Nuclear proliferation, biological experimentation, space exploration, sexual freedom, social injustices, and governmental manipulation have become commonplace. Because of their overwhelming implications, a tendency may exist to ignore or repress these and other current issues.

The complexity of life today can be so overwhelming that the need for security of one's private world may supersede the need for knowledge and involvement. It may be safer to remain entombed in comfort then to face, with determination and persistence, the disorder and discord around us. Withdrawal invites individuals to a state of perpetual immaturity.

However, the call to move forward is clear. We cannot hide. We cannot pretend that we can live within these private worlds without being impacted by society. Yet, we cannot depend entirely on either ourselves or others. Jesus told us, "Without me you can do nothing" and then laid out the beatitudes for our direction. This clarion invitation must be faced by each adult.

Yet, who is the adult?

The word itself is based on the Latin *adolescere,* which means to *grow up.* This definition is a dynamic one, implying a continuous process. It suggests a beginning plus ongoing development heading toward wholeness and completeness. It indicates a continuum on which one step, one action, one experience leads to another. As these steps are taken, adults, through reflection, prayer, and study begin and continue to discern the uniqueness of Self, of the cocreative powers within, and the goals towards which they continuously need to strive. Thus, they move on their journey of *growing up.*

On one hand, this journey is traveled alone when each person, consciously or unconsciously, sets a destination and takes the necessary steps to reach it. It is traveled alone since growth requires personal responsibility for decision, behavior, and accountability. Those who allow themselves to be dominated by others and have given up this responsibility have opted to remain immature.

Journeying is demanding since it compels determined movement toward maturation and *growing up.* Children start out in embryo not only in physical but also in emotional, intellectual, personal, sexual, social, and spiritual development. Their growth into adulthood is irregular, uneven, and unique. As life progresses, challenges become more complex. Integration and the need for wholeness surface into consciousness. By the time of young adulthood, discovering and embracing the intricacies of the Self, dealing with one's weaknesses,

4

living in community without permitting domination or manipulation; and sharing and sacrificing self when that is needed and appropriate begin to demand attention.

Through experience, the irregularity and unevenness may shift to a balance. There is a tendency within the individual towards integration over fragmentation. The emotional, intellectual, personal, physical, sexual, social, and spiritual aspects of the Self tend to keep pace with one another. In time, however, one aspect takes precedence over another but, eventually, the interplay of all brings focus to experience and helps to lead the person towards wholeness. It is important to note that fragmentation can be present without derailing the journey. However, the person accepts and seeks to integrate this fragmentation.

Ongoing movement and creativity are usually assured when the outer and inner worlds of an individual become interdependent. This interdependence brings with it a vision of something greater and outside of Self, a sense of power as well as of tolerance, and a realistic assessment of personal abilities and limitations.

On the other hand, no one travels the journey alone.

There are many companions and they influence the traveler in varied ways. Present are individuals of many ages, competencies, gifts, and dreams. Present also are persons at various stages.

Adult beginners look forward expectantly to what is to come. Those who have journeyed awhile are like the two-faced Janus, looking back to what has already been and looking forward to what is yet to come. Then there are those whose journeys are almost completed. They relate to their past to understand where they have come from and how they have gotten to this juncture. They set about the task of unfinished business. When travelers are aware of one another, they benefit from the experience and wisdom of all of the journeyers.

For the Christian, the constant companion is Jesus Christ. He is the friend, the challenger, the teacher, the lover. As mentor, he understands the needs of each individual and makes demands, calls forth courage, offers himself as model, bears burdens, listens and understands. He seeks a response through a message that is frequently difficult to accept.

Because he loves us totally, he asks for our unconditional love. Because he is meek and humble of heart, he requests the laying aside of pride and arrogance. Because he is just, he petitions a change of heart that eliminates oppressive and violent actions. Even when ignored, he walks silently along the way.

Characteristics of Maturation

When we examine the research of developmental psychologists, we note a striking similarity. They acknowledge that adulthood is not a static stage achieved at some period and then encased in solidarity and security. Regardless of the descriptions that each researcher uses, they are based on a dynamism, an energy, and the unlimited possibility found within each person. Maturation, individuation, life patterns, passages, process, journey, passover, and generativity are terms found consistently in their literature. Development and *growing up* are as magnets luring an individual to an ultimate goal.

Previous to reaching legal adulthood, an individual grows from birth to childhood to adolescence. This is a pattern that is recognizable and acceptable. However, this movement toward fulfillment is not as evident once adulthood is reached. It is important, therefore, to acknowledge the characteristics toward maturation that are present in adults. The purpose here is to outline in broad strokes what some of the researchers indicate is a continuous movement toward wholeness.

Erik Erikson claims that progression is sequential but is not dependent upon a specific age. He outlines this progression in the following steps: the need for trust, autonomy, initiative, industry, identity, intimacy, generativity, and ego integrity. As a person's identity is formed, self-confidence and a disassociation from roles surfaces. One develops faith in Self and acknowledges limitations, thus avoiding confusion springing from others' expectations. One is ready to risk closeness, to offer thoughts, feelings, and experiences to another. There is a concern, through generativity, to leave something of Self behind. This is done through parenting and creativity whereby one leaves a legacy to upcoming generations of works of art, music, writing, and service.

At the end of life, a person has the potential for ego integrity whereby one accepts the only life cycle with a sense of dignity and fulfillment in spite of failure or despair. The final achievement is the assent to death.

Abraham Maslow speaks of a direction toward self-actualization (maturity) based on a keen perception of reality; an increased acceptance of Self, others and nature; a great freshness of appreciation; and an increased need for privacy and detachment. His progression begins with meeting the basic physical, psychological, and emotional needs and then moves to self-esteem and esteem for others. It culminates in the creativity of self-expression.

Maslow believes that, because of circumstances in life, individuals sometimes are found locked into one level of existence. At times, unless someone else helps them, these individuals remain on their levels, unaware that life might have another reality.

According to Maslow, it is not possible to skip levels. Each level prepares one for the next. Yet, when individuals move from one level to another, they do it at their own pace and their own rhythm. Each person progresses individually and so there is no need to compare, compete, or model someone else's rhythm. An individual can remain at a particular level indefinitely, refining and developing skills. One cannot be induced, shoved, or threatened onto another level. The rate of development cannot be accelerated, or even predicted, because of the infinite variety of circumstances that enter into a person's life.

One can expect to find obstacles on each level. Poor health, unemployment, catastrophic weather which damages or destroys, may consume the attention of an individual so that nothing else can be considered. At that point, satisfaction of physical needs becomes paramount.

The breakup of a marriage or friendship, the loss of a loved one by death, and separations of various kinds can keep one struggling with psychological and emotional needs even after physical needs have been satisfied. When one is engaged in such struggles, the probability of finding a breakthrough to a higher level seems slim. These negative factors can damage one's self-esteem and lead to distrust, fear, uncertainty, insecurity, and hatred of Self and others. When one is trapped in this sort of whirlpool, one experiences mostly defeat, depression, uselessness, and meaninglessness. The effort to be creative, self-assured, and self-accepting is blocked.

Awareness of one's situation is important. If a person seems to be battling through a fog or sinking into a quagmire, it becomes imperative to have a friend, a mentor, or a spiritual director who can offer a helping hand, support, presence, and love. When such a person helps a struggling individual sort out events, reflect upon experiences, and plot solutions, then some semblance of order, tranquility, and peace within Self is possible. The movement forward and upward begins again.

Maslow's top level deals with peak experiences which are periods of great personal impact. Each peak experience coordinates all that has gone before and brings it to a summit. A peak experience helps one to enjoy an event to the utmost but it also requires a withdrawal of Self to reflect upon and assimilate the impact of that event in order to determine present meaning and future direction.

Peak experiences are the glorious moments of one's life. They take a person to the mountain top where the air is rarified and the view magnificent. Here time seems to stop. One is so overwhelmed, awed, and immersed that the person may feel disembodied.

Peak experiences are distinctive because they are so memorable but they are rare and far between. One cannot live on a mountain top too long, for no growth takes place there. The verdant fruit lies on the inclines and in the valley. Before one can get to the peak, one must have walked, worked, and been nourished down below.

For Carl Jung, the Swiss psychotherapist who spent decades studying the personality, maturation is the process of becoming whole through the integration of the opposites within the person. Integration begins when the ego, that outward part of the Self that is projected to others, slowly commences to give way to the inward self, hidden within the unconscious. Jung defines Self as the creativity of God working within. In biblical terms, it might be expressed as *the kingdom of God within us.*

Jung also believes that the task of individuation (maturation) originates in childhood and is operative throughout a lifetime. He likens the process to continuous birthing and dying: dying to the womb to birth into physical life, dying to childhood to birth into young adulthood, dying to young adulthood to birth into middle age, and then dying to physical life to birth into a new form of life.

He also divides a lifetime into halves with the first half focusing on the outer world of skill development, identity, relationships, family, career, social life, and achievement wherein the ego dominates in its various roles and masks. He sees the task of the second half of life as centering on the inner world where a person deals with the issues of meaning, identity, and integration.

This inner world is the life of mystery, symbol, and ritual. It is dominated by the unconscious wherein the shadow, the anima/animus, various archetypes, and personal and collective memories and experiences reside. It is from the unconscious that dreams surface as God's language to alert individuals of their spiritual needs. It is here that the various polarities of life are assimilated: the pain and the joy, the tearing apart and the healing, the hatred and the love, the struggle and the victory. It is the abyss in which fears and insecurities roost their tentacles which must be shaken loose to allow for freedom and innocence.

For Jung, when a person develops a relationship with the unconscious, individuation moves steadily along. A primary task, then, is to bring the shadow into the light, to become friends with it, to embrace it, to love it and thus to integrate it into the personality. The shadow contains the evil possibilities within us which sometimes surface in dreams, fantasies, and various symbols. It also contains the good possibilities which are sometimes rejected, primarily out of fear of the responsibilities which might ensue if one were to develop and use them.

Jung underscores the need for the animus/anima to become friends. The animus is the masculine within us; the anima is the feminine. Both of these are at odds with one another in the unconscious. Integration lies in accepting and integrating the qualities of the opposite sex: for the man, the nurturing and receptivity of the feminine; for the woman, the creativity and aggressiveness of the masculine. This integration can lead to a freer expression of intimacy on the conscious level.

8

Individuation, for Jung, is a lifelong process. It is an ongoing inner unfolding toward a distant goal. It is becoming a completed and unique person. In the process, the ego contacts the Self, the center of unknown totality, for its source of energy and strength. The Self, on the other hand, needs the ego, for the Self's emergence takes place through the expression of the ego. However, internal battles occur when the ego resists the Self in its efforts to organize life around itself. Since the perpetuation of its own egocentric pattern is important, it sees integration with the Self as a threat.

Summary

In reviewing the characteristics on the journey towards maturation, several factors emerge. Chief among these are:

1. Adults, throughout all of life, are capable of learning new behaviors.
2. They can meet the challenge of the various crises in their lives, reflect upon them, and determine the kinds of changes that are needed and wanted.
3. At the passage points of the birthing and dying, a struggle occurs because values and goals change, and it may be some time before a period of tranquility sets in.
4. Even though crises may seem overpowering, adults are quite capable of dealing with them, generating the psychic, emotional, and spiritual energies needed to reach another level of development.
5. There needs to be an interplay between the external events and their internal assimilation so that, through reflection and prayer, an adult can come to terms with life at each stage.
6. The rhythm that researchers outline does not necessarily apply to all individuals, since persons have their own pulse and uniqueness. There is no need for concern if one appears to be *out of synch* with the timeliness suggested.
7. It is possible that some major life tasks will never be attempted because of specific lifestyles, e.g., an unmarried person may not need to deal with raising a family.
8. The maturation process is lifelong.
9. The challenges, difficulties, and crises of life are important, if not essential, ingredients in the maturation process.

Christian Maturity

If the above are the characteristics of adulthood and maturity, then how can they be applied to a Christian seeking wholeness? What dimension does Christianity add to adult maturity (holiness)?

A Christian is not different from any other person, for humanity is everyone's common denominator. Yet, when individuals become Christians, they inherit a special dimension—the privilege of having Jesus as a comrade. In addition, Christians band together in common worship, mission, and service. They admonish and support, they love and are loved as they seek to live out the directives of their leader. They are lured to wholeness because of their personal call and the guidance and sustenance available from all those moving toward the same goal.

Evelyn E. Whitehead and James D. Whitehead, in their book *Christian Life Patterns*, trace the development of holiness as it occurs over the lifespan. They believe that holiness is success at living and that both psychological and religious maturity will be achieved in a creative response to loss and failure. They claim that a healthy response necessitates a reintegration and reconciliation of the adult with one's Self and with the community. The crisis of loss and failure becomes a religious event when the person recognizes in the experience the challenging and supportive presence of God.

Religious maturity, according to the Whiteheads, is the ability to be loving and generative. It is to discover a gift within the unexpected turns and crosses of adult life. They emphasize that growth occurs *toward* adulthood rather than *in* adulthood. They suggest that self-identity leads to discipleship; that ability to love and to give of oneself generates charity; and that the capacity for responsible care is lived out in stewardship.

They see the Christian gospel as essential, since it is the good news about the crisis of Jesus Christ when he underwent his passion, death, and resurrection, modeling for us a pattern for our lives.

James W. Fowler discerns distinct stages in the development of faith. His message is twofold: children are not *little adults* who should behave as adults, and adults have not *made it* but can continue to grow in wisdom, morality, and fidelity.

Although Fowler defines faith as an ordered, consistent way of looking at the world, his research reveals areas that are helpful for growth in Christian maturity.

He sees transition points as times when the center of things seems to fall away and the world is disorderly. This is the period when an individual needs to recenter life on a new value or on a more adequate understanding of God and our place in the universe.

Fowler indicates that the emergence into a new stage of faith can be gradual, yet, sometimes events come together in a sudden, distinct moment of enlightenment. It is at times like these that we need to acknowledge that ours is not a private faith but that a community of shared values has touched us. Therefore, faith is the total framework by which we live and are related to other people and the world. It underlines the way we discover meaning in life and understand our existence.

Young people become acquainted with primal faith through the love, trust, hope, and courage that is offered them through others and which, through these experiences, is also called forth from within themselves.

As imagination develops and helps children to form images, they develop intuitive faith and become aware of death and sex. They lack a rational understanding at this time, but they have a fundamental loyalty and trust.

Later, logic takes over and begins to both shape and complement the yet-undisciplined imagination. Emphasis on the past, present, and future underlines this stage of faith. The older child and adolescent develop broader loyalties to God, nature, and people. Storytelling becomes significant.

In the synthetic faith stage, not only are stories central, but individuals also begin to examine the meaning of these stories. Now an entirely new worldview surfaces and crises and contradictions lead to a deeper understanding of life. Persons in this stage become concerned with identity and cling to those groups or individuals who affirm it.

In young adulthood or later, the move is into individuative faith. During this time, the conviction surfaces that, because of individual experiences, each of us is unique and that we are not totally dependent upon another for meaning, definition, or identity. It is during this period that symbols and their personal meaning become important. What happens, however, is that some people never come to this stage, for they cannot let go of the image that others have of them.

As persons progress, they come, in conjunctive faith, to appreciate the mysteries of themselves and others and to find meaning in contradiction and paradox. Justice becomes important and it is possible that separation from family and friends may follow when both do not have the same values.

Fowler claims that the final stage, that of universalizing faith, is very rare. These are the individuals who feel at one with all of humanity, who are willing to suffer for others. They are sometimes perceived as being disloyal to a particular institution and so may be imprisoned or martyred. It is these people who point to something much greater than themselves.

Comparing this last stage to that of other theorists, Fowler sees it as similar to Maslow's self-actualizing stage and Erikson's stage of integrity. He emphasizes that each period has the potential for wholeness, grace, and integrity and carries the necessary strengths sufficient for crisis situations as well as for life's blessings.

And what of Jesus Christ? What has he to say?

This rabboni, this master teacher, has from the very beginning, invited us to follow him. He is the way. He leads us into the desert as well as to the mountain top. He challenges us to become a seed, to die, to remain at times alone, to bear much fruit. He asks us to love unconditionally, to strive for perfection, to give up our hard hearts and our deaf ears.

He models prayer as he retreats to caves and deserts, as he agonizes in a garden and on crossed beams of wood. He urges us to take up our crosses and then he tells us about the mansions which God has prepared for us.

He blesses us as we care for the poor, the oppressed, the victims of circumstance and injustice. He petitions us to accept persecution, to become lowly, to give up possessions. He wants us to put our light on a mountain top, to be salt for the earth.

What seems significant for a Christian seeking maturity, individuation, or holiness is the role that God plays in the process. We understand God because Jesus Christ, the Son, became a human being and by living, aching, feeling, serving, loving, and praying in our midst became a prototype.

Born as a baby, Jesus grew in age, wisdom, and grace. He developed as any child and youth in Nazareth and then, in young adulthood, started his public search for meaning.

Being affirmed by his father at the Jordan gave him the strength to plunge ahead. Recognizing the task before him, Jesus entered the wilderness to spend time alone. Here he plunged into the chasm of himself to seek the courage he needed to face the demons, both within and without. The father was there to support and energize him, offering Jesus the power he needed to achieve his destiny.

Leaving the desert, Jesus chose intimate friends for his inner circle. But he also mingled easily with the downtrodden and the powerful, the curious and the sincere, sinners and the virtuous. He plodded the mountains and valleys of Galilee, fished and swam in the lake of Chinnereth, told stories around campfires and on hillsides, sought out and healed the crazed and the handicapped. He mixed with centurions and mothers-in-law, with Pharisees and prostitutes. He slept in caves and under the stars and succumbed to his yearning for Jerusalem.

The time he spent in the holy city was usually a stormy one. He preached his message in the outer court of the temple to both the learned and the ignorant. Since he was one of the most-wanted men in Jerusalem, he welcomed his hideout in Bethany.

Eventually, he signed his death warrant by raising his friend from the dead. The die was cast when he rode down the slope of the Mount of Olives on the back of an ass. One of the most-wanted men was ready to be apprehended. But before his capture, he gave us the gift of his body and blood for our sustenance and hope.

He was seized, tortured, sentenced, and killed. His convulsive cry, "My God, my God, why have you forsaken me?" rang over the hillside. All nature held its breath when he whispered his final acceptance. "It is finished" did not put closure to his life, for he rose and is among us.

His was an ordinary but exceptional life as he matured and developed, consciously aware of its meaning. If a researcher would have used Jesus as a subject, he probably would have been delighted with the findings. In the process of maturation, Jesus *grew up* searching for identity, dealing with his shadow, being comfortable with the women and men in his life, and generating a life force that would continue until the end of time.

Our hearts burn within us as we journey, for the Lord Jesus is with us. He does not judge nor rebuff, send away or ignore. He embraces us, gathers us as a mother hen gathers her chicks under her wings. We are protected, challenged, sent forth. By loving him, we love his father, mother. Neither chaos nor crisis can separate us from him.

If we are *to grow* in Christian maturity, then we need to be as ordinary and as exceptional as Jesus was. Our lives must be a march toward our destiny. In this forward movement we, too, need to enter our abysses to discover the unsuspected treasures therein. We need to welcome our crises, accept our pain, deal with new challenges, demands, and decisions.

We also need to be aware of the others on the journey and join hands with these travelers. With such a community, the stride toward wholeness (holiness) is assured. That is what makes the journey so enticing.

Reclaiming Meaning: A Response to The Mature Christian Adult

Fred Eyerman

Maturation is a lifelong, personal, often tumultuous search for meaning. It begins at birth and continues, through somewhat defined stages and critical turning points, until death. It is a process that is inner-directed and must be traversed individually, but which is assisted, sometimes necessarily so, by others. It is an ideal that is never reached but a goal that we are urged restlessly toward. It is further dimensioned, for a Christian, by the model and call of Jesus Christ, by a common tradition, and by the support and challenge of a community of fellow travelers toward wholeness. In sum, it is the journey each of us must travel in search of our authentic self, to be who we are called to be through the uniqueness of our birth and the grace-filled moments of daily life.

These are just some of the insights I found in Loretta Girzaitis's lead article, "The Mature Christian Adult." Using ideas from developmental psychologists—Erikson, Maslow, Jung, the Whiteheads, Fowler—Girzaitis offers primarily a description of the process of maturation, specifically Christian maturation. Her article concludes with a meditationlike presentation of Jesus Christ as model of this process.

For each of the past 17 years I have been professionally involved in some aspect of assisting adult learning. I am increasingly impressed with the need to develop more flexible, open, and comprehensive systems to support the lifelong learning/maturing process outlined in the Girzaitis article. Specific responses are suggested for the Church. Do we need parish and diocesan systems that are *learning communities?* How do we develop from offering *series of courses* to providing environments in which learning is a priority for most and especially evident in leadership, where all persons are invited to participate, and where people, together, are caring for each other's growth needs and challenging each other to express the Christian message in day-to-day life? In identifying some of the implications of the Girzaitis article for adult religious educators, I would like to offer seven recommendations for our educational systems.

1. Set *priorities* that enable the allocation of resources in support of lifelong learning systems.

Within the Catholic tradition, the American bishops have issued several statements in support of lifelong and adult formation. *Serving Life and Faith*[1] is a comprehensive statement from the USCC Department of Education about the nature and importance of adult religious education within the Church's life and mission. I believe it is necessary reading for the Catholic adult educator and others in planning concrete responses to the challenges of Christian maturation. The Church, at all levels, should seriously assist in the translation of these positive statements into concrete and adequate strategies and resources that support learning for faith maturity.

---

[1]USCC Department of Education, *Serving Life and Faith: Adult Religious Education and the American Catholic Community* (Washington, D.C.: USCC Office of Publishing and Promotion Services, 1986).

2. Set *goals* that are comprehensive and clear enough to support the multifarious, lifelong maturation needs of diverse and changing individuals.

Lifelong learning addresses many needs at many levels. It can be a very confusing programming problem. Needed, I believe, are some general goals that provide a framework within which specific objectives and strategies can be worked out. Girzaitis's article suggests that maturation is the lifelong search for meaning. If so, Leon McKenzie offers what I believe is one of the clearest statements of purpose for educators.

In the lead article of the *Handbook of Adult Religious Education*, he writes that the purpose of religious education and religious educators is to help people

(1) *acquire* meaning,
(2) *explore* and *expand* meaning, and
(3) *express* meaning effectively.[2]

In today's Church, I would add the need to help others *reclaim* meaning. Many adults have lost touch with the main tenets of their Christian tradition. I believe the current interest in catechisms stems from this need. As an option to catechisms, we might want to look again at Fr. Karl Rahner's use of "short formulas of the faith."[3]

In Denver we developed a program called "Christians in Search" that was structured around a "short formula." Using a highly participatory small group model, the program sought to help adults reclaim their basic meaning system. A good percentage of the participants, ten years later, are still involved in their own ongoing faith formation and are active in service to others.

3. Develop *unified learning systems* that support the ongoing development of each individual from cradle-to-grave.

This implication ties into the priority issue. Our present systems are segmented into various levels—child, youth, adult. The most important challenge today may be for each level to play down personal agendas in order to work together to develop truly lifelong learning systems. Individual growth, while never smooth, follows a continuum

---

[2]Nancy T. Foltz, Editor, *Handbook of Adult Religious Education* (Birmingham, Alabama: Religious Education Press, 1986), "The Purposes and Scope of Adult Religious Education," Leon McKenzie, pp. 10–13.
[3]Eberhard, K. D., "Rahner on Religious Education," *Thought* (1973) 48:190, pp. 404–415.

of stages. Our support systems must be able to respond effectively to this continuous search for meaning.

A possible model for a unified, continuous system was developed by Harold Shane in *The Educational Significance of the Future*.[4] Shane was suggesting alternative futures to the public educational system. His suggestion of a lifelong, "seamless curriculum" of formal and informal (what he calls the paracurriculum) learning resources offers a starting point for our own development of learning systems.

Counseling or brokering services within the system would be a major part of such a lifelong structure. A helpful resource is the Community Education Movement[5] and its experience with addressing comprehensive learning needs. We are challenged to determine how we can transform our dioceses and parishes into lifelong *learning communities*.

4. Develop lifelong learning systems that are *flexible*.

One major conclusion of the Girzaitis article was the importance of *passage points* and the variability of such experiences (age, intensity, characteristics of) for each person. The most teachable moments in a person's life may be when he or she is negotiating these critical passages. It is then, primarily, that a person needs assistance. According to Maslow, the presence or absence of timely assistance may determine further development. Many of our present systems are not flexible enough to meet dynamic, individual growth needs. How many parish adult religious education programs are finalized by September with little in the way of counseling or brokering services to help persons with new or nonprogrammed needs? Here are some suggestions:

(1) Adult educators should appreciate the variability of adult growth patterns and apply this understanding to concrete programming. A resource that explains major patterns and offers specific programming suggestions is *The Handbook of Adult Religious Education*.[6] Presented is a series of chapters on working with young, middle-aged, older, single parent, and separated and divorced adults as well as with adults in death-related circumstances.

[4]Harold G. Shane, *The Educational Significance of the Future* (Bloomington, Indiana: Phi Delta Kappa, Inc., 1973), "Learning Designs for Tomorrow," chapter IV, pp. 59–94.
[5]Contact the National Community Education Association, 119 North Payne Street, Alexandria, Virginia 22314 (703-683-6232). See Jack D. Minzey and Clyde E. LeTarte, *Community Education: From Program to Process* (Midland, Michigan: Pendell Publishing Company, 1979) or Mary Richardson Boo and Larry E. Decker, *The Learning Community* (Alexandria, Virginia: National Community Education Association, 1985).
[6]Foltz, op. cit., chapters 3 to 9.

(2) Educational brokering,[7] counseling, and spiritual direction should become more prevailing styles for adult religious educators. We are in the business of enabling growth within a meaning system. We should be capable of helping individuals respond to the key experiences in *their* lives in dialog and tension with the Christian vision and the *signs of our times.*

(3) In support of (2) above, each diocese should consider development of a computer-based data bank of available resources, especially persons and programs. Procedures could be established to tie this into an effective clearinghouse service to area educators. Often the best response to a need is not local development of another program but use of resources that already exist. Individual educators usually do not have the time to keep in touch with all resources. An effective clearinghouse service can provide responses to many needs while reducing time, cost, and unnecessary duplication of services. In difficult economic times, this may be a necessity.

5. Develop lifelong learning systems that are *open and accessible to all persons.*

According to the developmental psychologists, *all* persons have the inner urge toward wholeness. Are we limiting our efforts to the 10 percent (13 percent for all adult education in 1981 according to the U.S. Department of Education's National Center for Education Statistics) who respond to formal programs? These are apt to be white, middle-class, and educated. Shouldn't we consciously adjust our systems so that they are welcoming to any member of our communities when their need is present? I believe that is what Fowler[8] is emphasizing when he suggests that our congregations need to become environments of *care* so that they can become also environments of *vocation,* of challenge and transformation. *Hospitality* and openness to the diversity within our individual communities are essential ingredients in support of the lifelong maturation of all members.

Our local communities need gathering times and places when and where new people can gain entry to them. (*Be welcomed* is too threatening for some!) Some parishes are now introducing community learning evenings or weekends open to the entire congregation. These

[7]See James M. Hefferman, Francis U. Macy and Donn F. Vickers, *Educational Brokering: A New Service for Adult Learners* (Syracuse, New York: National Center for Educational Brokering, 1976).

[8]James W. Fowler, *Faith Development and Pastoral Care* (Philadelphia, Pennsylvania: Fortress Press, 1987), part of the Theology and Pastoral Care series edited by Don S. Browning. See, especially, chapter 7, "Pastoral Care, Faith Development, Public Church," pp. 113–120. This entire book is recommended reading for addressing the maturation question through transformed learning systems.

events include classes but can also offer counseling services, faith sharing groups, or just the opportunity to meet together informally for a cup of coffee.

6. Provide *educational leadership* that is *transformational.*

For a description of this style, read David Thomas's article in this publication. One of the primary skills of *transformational leadership* is *listening.* We need to be capable, caring, and open persons who walk with others in their time of need. Parenthetically, an ongoing process of *informal* listening may be the most effective approach to that perennial stumbling block of adult religious education and an essential factor in helping adults mature (needs assessment).

7. Be comfortable with *the questioning mind.*

There are many other implications one could draw out of an article on Christian maturation. One not to be overlooked is the necessity of knowing and applying sound adult education principles in our work. In this regard, I would highly recommend Stephen Brookfield's book, *Understanding and Facilitating Adult Learning.*[9]

I would like to end with some brief comments on the necessary role of *doubt* in the process of Christian maturation. M. Scott Peck, in his new book, *The Different Drum,*[10] suggests four stages of development: chaotic/antisocial, formal/institutional, *skeptic/individual* and mystic/communal. Doubt is a necessary stage on the journey to wholeness. How open are we, as Church, as educators, to allow persons to doubt? Peck, in quite strong words, believes that "one of the two greatest sins of our sinful Christian church has been its discouragement of doubt through the ages." We need to enable people to ask questions, to doubt, to struggle with life issues, to not only bring our tradition into dialog with day-to-day reality, but also to question our tradition. One of the major trends in the current Catholic Education Futures Project is a call for training in critical-thinking skills. To grow, people must question! How we handle this issue may determine how far our people and communities proceed on their lifelong journey toward meaning and Christian maturity.

---

[9]Stephen D. Brookfield, *Understanding and Facilitating Adult Learning: A Comprehensive Analysis of Principles and Effective Practices* (San Francisco, California: Jossey-Bass, Inc., Publishers, 1986).
[10]M. Scott Peck, M.D., *The Different Drum: Community Making and Peace* (New York: Simon and Schuster, 1987), Chapter IX, "Patterns of Transformation," pp. 186–208. Peck's four stages are outlined on page 188. The quote I use starts at the bottom of page 199 and continues to the top of page 200.

Leadership in Adult Religious Education

David M. Thomas

Childhood is all too brief. Adolescence is a passing moment. By contrast, adulthood generally accompanies us the longest on our journey through time. Most appropriate then is our growing awareness of the importance of the adult's life of faith in the Church. In heightening this awareness, the Second Vatican Council affirmed the importance of full participation for all members of the Church. There is an essential link between participation and adulthood. Indeed, increased participation in life, wherever its setting, is the hallmark of adulthood.

The achievement of deeper and more meaningful participation requires an understanding of *what's happening*. Further, people need to know not only the ingredients of the present moment, but also what has gone before to make this moment pregnant with rich possibilities. Full learning also includes a knowledge of those negatives in life that destroy individuals and communities so that we do not recreate the hurts and failures of the past.

Prior to Vatican II the Church was content to supply only a modicum of formal opportunities for adults to deepen personal knowledge of their faith. Today, however, it is clear there is a new valuing of adult religious education. The United States Catholic Conference Department of Education endorsed this move in language persuasive and urgent with the issuance of *Serving Life and Faith* that should be listed among the most important religious education documents of this century. The value of adult learning has been affirmed, the explanation for its importance has been articulated. It is now time to translate words into action; possibility into actual opportunity. This will be a major task within the Church for the decade of the 90s.

To inaugurate new organizational priorities in the Church, to offer unprecedented opportunities for personal and communal growth, we urgently need strong and committed leadership. Change does not happen spontaneously. It is not based on mysterious forces. And if it appears otherwise, usually this means we are simply not aware of all that is going on. From a functional perspective, good leadership is that action within the community which initiates vital newness, catalyzes appropriate change, maintains proper direction, announces needed correction, and empowers each member of the community toward reaching a fuller portion of life's benefits. The task of the Church's leadership is to help us change from concentrating almost exclusively on the young, to supporting more actively adult, lifelong learning.

We know a fair amount about leaders, particularly from an historical perspective. Unfortunately, we know a lot less about leadership. These are the conclusions of James MacGregor Burns, author of *Leadership*, a Pulitzer Prize winning book on this topic. Facing this void of knowledge, Burns offers a descriptive distinction which we will take as a starting point for our analysis of leadership in adult religious education.

He argues that there are two types of leadership. The most common kind of leadership he describes as *transactional leadership*. It is based on an act of exchange where the leader gives something (knowledge, skill, insight, direction, etc.) to the follower. The traditional distinction between teacher and pupil is based on transactional exchange. A political leader may exchange promises for votes. A football coach may exchange instruction and motivation for touchdowns. A clergyperson may exchange moving sermons for religious conversions. Burns notes that our common use of the notion of leadership is rooted in these kinds of transactions. The leaders act in ways that bring about appropriate responses in the follower(s). Better leaders are paid to generate more significant responses.

A second kind of leadership, more subtle, yet perhaps more important than the first, he terms *transformational leadership*. An indication that transactional leadership is happening is when *followers* are being changed into *leaders*. Transactional leadership frees, empowers, develops, releases, redeems, launches, opens, and liberates. Good parenting works on the principle of transformational leadership. It assists the child to reach adulthood. The parent rejoices when the child is able to have his or her own thoughts and can make good decisions rooted in personal responsibility.

Part of the process inherent in transformational leadership is that the leader is available to the follower as a role model, as a witness to those events and processes which brought the leader to a position of authority within the community. The leader embodies in some way "the way, the truth, and the life" of the community. Obviously, Jesus was a transformational leader. He led by example.

Let us now reflect on adult religious education in the church and draw some implications of these distinctions between transactional leadership and transformational leadership. I will begin by affirming the need for *both* kinds of leadership.

As was already mentioned, the most common form of leadership is transactional. Applied to settings of adult religious education, it would be apparent in programs where information is communicated. An example is a program which updates people on new and expanded meanings of lay ministry or where new skills are developed, such as

20

in training volunteers to take communion to the sick. Given the changing structure of church life, especially as the reforms of Vatican II are expanded throughout the Church, we will need informed and competent leadership to offer people knowledge and skills appropriate to the new opportunities of participation in today's Church.

Transformational leadership is needed where personal spiritual growth and/or small group development is the central focus. With both these priorities immensely important today, we clearly need this kind of empowering presence at every level of church life.

What special traits might we observe in the transformational leader? I would underscore three: humility, empathy, and sincerity. Humility is that virtue which grounds one in the truth. Humility allows the educator to affirm both what is known and unknown. It is the opposite of intellectual pride where one boasts of personal knowledge and uses that knowledge (however meager it might be) to support a position of superiority over those who lack the same knowledge. Isaac Newton, a genuine lifelong learner, once wrote, "I seem to have been only like a boy playing on the seashore and diverting myself in now and then finding a smoother pebble or prettier shell than ordinary, whilst the great ocean of truth lay undiscovered before me." Such humility always positions oneself as a learner, along with being a teacher. One remains in constant search of a better, more comprehensive grasp of the truth.

Empathy is that quality which brings one to know what is happening within another. Genuine empathy requires a quieting of one's interior noise to be able to hear the quiet sound of life within others. It is an expression of the ministry of listening. A leadership that listens in this way hears the pulse of life within the community and learns from that listening (and conversation) what is really needed to preserve and augment communal, religious vitality.

Sincerity values truth-telling. The original meaning of this word comes from the Latin, *sine cera* (without wax). It is the virtue of honesty which, in the sense of this essay, means that sincere leadership communicates exactly what it knows and what it fails to know. There is no pretense of knowing. This virtue also orients the community to a broad search for truth based on the assumption that no one person is in full possession of truth. It values inquiry and questioning and rejoices in all learning gains. This spirit of honest inquiry will be present in vital adult religious education programming. In itself, this approach to adult learning invites the active participation of all. It respects the hunger of the mind for truth.

Given the particular goal of adult religious education as the knowledge of God and the things of God, transformational leadership seems more attuned to approaching its subject matter with an openness appropriate to mystery. Christian discipleship is associated with the idea of discipline and learning. Being a disciple is to position oneself

21

as a learner before the mystery of God. *Everyone* in the Church is in that posture. I recall *stories of learning* told by bishops as they returned from the Second Vatican Council. They spoke of having returned to school, and, for the most part, it was a deeply enriching experience for them. They were changed in vision and conviction. Further, the more responsible bishops initiated diocesan-wide learning events for clergy and laity to learn about the wonderful insights of the council. Fresh air was blowing through the Church.

Recall, too, that many of the major medieval universities of Europe were established by the Church with theology serving as the integrative science of the schools. And those days are sometimes called the Dark Ages.

The Church is approaching its two-thousandth birthday. Through all the years its educational task has remained the same: communicate the truth, hope, and love of Jesus to *all* its members. A renewed emphasis on how all this is being brought ever deeper into the lives of its members has prompted the Church to underscore the importance of *lifelong* learning for all its members. We need in the Church the kind of leadership that values learning, that supports its processes, and that sees itself as a coparticipant in the adventure of learning. In other words, we need that kind of transformational leadership that brings the members of the Church to the level of leadership consonant with an *adult* sense of discipleship and vocation. I offer, therefore, a sampling of principles aimed at providing that special kind of leadership attuned to adults seeking the truth ever deep and ever challenging.

1. The Church is a complex social system. To ensure effective leadership in it, the leadership role must be borne by the whole community as much as by individual members. The Church is a community on the move; it is not just a Church of pilgrims. It is a Pilgrim Church.

As a learning Church, there should be regularly scheduled learning events. By way of illustration, in the past few years, the bishops of the United States have sponsored various national hearings which were designed to probe specific issues like peace and war, the economy, the role of women, and the concerns of the laity. The results were excellent, especially when one considered the newness of these events. It was a special joy to even participate in these gatherings. They must continue.

2. Effective leadership is consciously expressed by a vision of new possibilities. While an important principle of leadership is that it is a quality of the entire community, in many cases it begins within individual members. Within these individuals, a vision, a dream of new possibilities emerges. This is the prophetic side of leadership.

John XXIII came to it with his image of a renewed Church. Paul

22

VI captured it with his plea before the United Nations of a world without war. John Paul I communicated new life to the Church by the simple expression of a smile. John Paul II constantly reminds us of the dignity of the human person. Part of leadership is seeing, reminding, and announcing what many tend to overlook or forget.

Capturing the visionary side of church life is part of what's required of effective leadership. Individual leaders, therefore, need time to learn, reflect, pray, and focus upon those matters which most need to be learned by the community.

They create quiet time and open space within themselves to see what others miss because of the hectic pace of modern life. In a word, leaders in adult religious education should become contemplatives. They are not simply technicians producing educational programs. They, themselves, are *resources* or sources from which both program content and format can be drawn. They are not the exclusive source of programming, but they can and should *infiltrate* what's offered in a positive way.

3. In the field of adult learning, many developments have surfaced in recent years. In increasing numbers, adults are returning to school. Many people change careers in mid-life and seek more education. But most influential, I believe, is the good experience of both formal and informal learning which accompanies more people today than ever before. In some ways, even the middle class is a leisure class that has been exposed through education to many areas of knowledge once considered only the realm of an elite. Professional educators and learning theorists have approached this new population of learners with curiosity and have discovered through research important ideas for anyone assuming a leadership role in this field.

A quick sampling of resources would be: Stephen Brookfield's work on the development of critical reasoning; David Kolb's contributions in identifying learning styles; Malcolm Knowles excellent suggestions in the area of learning contracts; the collaborative work of Mary Field Belenky, Blythe McVicker Clinchy, Nancy Rule Goldberger, and Jill Mattuck Tarule in the area of women's ways of knowing; and the work of Alan Tough on independent learning projects.

Adult faith development is another area of advancing knowledge. The work of James Fowler on stages of faith development, the emperical research of Kenneth Stokes on adult faith, the philosophical inquiries of John Elias, the synthesizing efforts of Gabriel Moran, and the attention to adult faith from the feminist perspective of Sharon Parks, are helpful to leaders in this ever advancing area of church life.

So, effective leaders understand the forces shaping adult education today and are armed with a host of ideas and resources that enable them to effectively facilitate formal and informal learning.

23

4. Competent leaders possess an overall understanding of the major components of the content area under their leadership. Up to now, I have focused more on process than content. In my experience of adult educators, I have seen excellent approaches to format issues, but sometimes I have wondered whether the leaders were really knowledgeable in the content of a particular program.

Comprehensive educational activities usually contain an orientation toward reaching the total person. Under analysis, the areas demanding attention are commonly divided into the cognitive, the affective, and the skills-development area. Years ago, most attention was focused on content. "Get the material across" was the name of the game. The lecture method was perfect for that purpose because the presenter could control the exposition of content. All the material could be covered. I remember Thomas Groome once commenting that with that method the goal was admirably achieved. The material was covered, but it was not *uncovered* or *discovered* by the learners.

As strange as it may sound, educators began to wonder whether an excessive concern for content might get in the way of effective learning. With that in mind, *process* was discovered. And right on the heels of concern for process came a new appreciation of the effective dimensions of learning. An essential aspect of adult education, particularly in the area of religion, was how people *felt* about the program. Here I would like to register a gnawing complaint I have about a certain type of program commonly disguised as adult religious education, particularly some of the more popular programs. My complaint concerns the fact that they are offered and received as affective education. They are directed almost solely to the feeling area of life. People like these programs because they are made to *feel good* while participating. I don't want this to sound elitist or as a judgment against the central need for affective religious education. Nor do I want to reduce education to a purely cognitive realm. Yet I witness too many educational opportunities missed when only the feelings of people are addressed. Evaluations of programming should include hard questions on what people learned and not just on whether they liked the program.

In adult religious education, I would hope that a leader would have a broad, up-to-date understanding of the basic tenets of the faith. One should be reading current periodicals and books in areas touching the areas where one offers adult religious education. Finally, as one who educates in a particular church tradition, one should be aware of those issues currently debated and discussed in the Church and be able to provide people with wise guidance as to ways people can become more knowledgeable about these issues.

In conclusion, I believe that the discovery of lifelong learning in the Church is among the great discoveries of our time. Adulthood is a blessing for individuals and communities. While adulthood brings with it a loss of a certain naivete' about reality—for instance, everything now appears in shades of grey rather than black and white—this move allows one to enter the richness of the created world in a new way. Given truth's complexity and depth, one can never return to passivity in learning. The creation of a more adequate understanding summons forth an active involvement in learning. Most excitedly for me is that now the whole world becomes the textbook from which I read to find God's truth. Every day, every interpersonal encounter, every word I read, every sight I see, can become part of the learning process. I sense this has something very important to say about the Incarnation of God in created form and about how that event is still going on "for those who have eyes to see." Yet to open the eyes of the blind requires what we are calling *leadership*. Eyes used to being closed (especially in sleep) sometimes accept the invitation to *rise and shine* with no small degree of resentment. That is why, in part, efforts toward adult religious education are sometimes met with resistance. So, a final quality worth mentioning is that of courage. Valuing lifelong learning invites lifelong commitment, even in the face of difficulty.

Suggested Readings:

Belenky, Mary Field, et. al., *Women's Ways of Knowing: The Development of Self, Voice and Mind* (New York: Basic Books, 1986).

Brookfield, Stephen, *Developing Critical Thinkers: Challenging Adults to Explore Alternative Ways of Thinking and Acting* (San Francisco: Jossey-Bass, Inc., Publishers, 1987).

Burns, James MacGregor, *Leadership* (New York: Harper and Row, 1987).

Dykstra, Craig, and Parks, Sharon, Editors, *Faith Development and Fowler* (Birmingham, Alabama: Religious Education Press, 1986).

Elias, John, *The Foundations and Practice of Adult Religious Education* (Malabar, Florida: Robert Krieger Publishing, 1982).

Kolb, David, *Experiential Learning: Experience as Source of Learning and Development* (Englewood Cliffs, New Jersey: Prentice-Hall, 1984).

Knowles, Malcolm, *Using Learning Contracts* (San Francisco: Jossey-Bass, Inc., Publishers, 1986).

Leader as Manager? A Response to Leadership in Adult Religious Education

Jane Wolford Hughes

David Thomas provides us with a provocative view of leadership that captures the diverse competencies of the effective Adult Religious Education (ARE) leader. He wisely places the leader in a situation of change and acknowledges the struggle inherent in the continual grappling with the reality of life. I especially appreciate the clean-cut distinctions between the two types of leadership—the transactional and transformational—and his use and support of each in specific situations. I hope his defense of a sound and comprehensive knowledge of content presented in appropriate formats—formal and informal, cognitive and affective—will confront biased ARE leaders to scramble out of their ruts and use an intelligent variety of formats.

David makes a good point about too many programs, packaged and locally designed, which address only the feelings of people. We do the learners a great disservice when we stroke them but never challenge them. A combination of the two makes for a deeper and more lasting learning experience.

Hooray for David's bibliography! He invites the reader into the current world of thinking which limbers the mind to make some leaps and take some risks. I will supplement his list with a few additions.

Faced with such a comprehensive rendition, you may perhaps wonder what I will add to it. In order not to be repetitive, I will offer the pragmatic view of the practitioner. I will attempt to build a frame around David's picture—holding it together, defining it further. We will briefly examine the leader as administrator/manager, collaborator, and entrepreneur.

Perhaps it is because we come from two different worlds of Adult Religious Education—academic and practitioner—that we see things differently. Before I begin the *frame*, I would like to situate us in the context of ARE as I see it, which is not quite as rosy as David's view.

I am not without hope but think ARE, as a separate discipline, may be in for rough times which gives us further cause to talk about the importance of well-trained, tough-minded, committed, and focused ARE leaders who recognize the problems and are prepared to deal with them.

The Adult Religious Education movement in the United States has made steady, if slow, progress in the past 20 years. However, despite

26

the dedicated and often inspired leadership, its growth, in the immediate past and present, has been responsive to the commitment, apathy, ignorance, or fear of many forces within the Church. In some areas, we have seen leaps forward only to have the pendulum crash backwards. In others, it is fixed in dead center, with nothing happening. In still others, it moves in the opposite direction, calling itself adult education but trivializing its effects by lack of consistency with the principles of ARE. Where the climate is hospitable and the leadership strong, there are groups of adults freely engaged in thinking, questioning, arguing, reevaluating the meaning of being a disciple of Jesus Christ, and preparing themselves to maturely deal with questions that haven't even been asked.

Because of this unsettled state, I'm not as positive as David that "lifelong learning in the Church is among the greatest discoveries of our time." It could be. With due respect to our efforts, I doubt that it has been properly mined, but I am optimistic that the motherlode of its potential will be discovered.

When we look back over the past, hindsight tells us a few things we should concentrate on in the future. Among them, these come foremost to mind:

1. greater integration and recognition of ARE in the church structure and systems through advocacy and collaboration,
2. increased accountability for quality control in design and delivery,
3. conscious anticipation of new trends.

I cite these to situate the leader in real circumstances that give reason for my emphasis on certain skills I believe are important in the development of the ARE leader. In the past, our training for ARE has been focused on content and especially on the nurturing role of ministering to the adult learner as facilitator/teacher and program planner. Not as much attention has been given to the administrative/ managerial aspects of the job. What can be done to bring about greater integration and recognition of ARE in the church structures and systems?

Despite all of the talk about ARE's importance and its primacy in the educational schema, I do not see this stance reflected in budgets nor on organizational charts. In fact, more structures are absorbing the education of adults into total religious education offices; some are cutting back on staffing and the autonomy of ARE. While it may make the charts neater and the bottom line fatter, it puts an additional responsibility upon the director of religious education who is already juggling an overload. Furthermore, if the management style of the diocese or parish is authoritarian or top-down, the shift places the

ARE leader one level further away from the decisionmaker(s) and diminishes the vitality and urgency of the ARE message.

As we project into the future, it seems prudent to provide management training for the ARE leader both in advocacy and in collaboration with others in the Church, in the community, and in other churches. Training in advocacy prepares the leader to speak for, represent, defend, and negotiate. If when decisions are being made on budgets, staffing, and structure, there is no one present with strong convictions, vested interest, solid reasons, and proof of both need and past success of ARE, who can blame the decisionmakers for minimizing it?

In order to be accomplished advocates, leaders need to understand the system that they address. Therefore, it is necessary for ARE leaders to understand the differences in ecclesial models and be able to define and adjust to the one with which they will work. Whether they agree with the philosophy of the model or not is not the issue. Advocacy is not a one-shot attempt but a long-term relationship. It is a grave but avoidable mistake to underestimate or ignore the power structure and to not be sensitive to how it works. Among other skills, the leader should learn conflict resolution, dealing with power, and skills in communication, persuasion, and negotiation.

Advocacy need not be the sole responsibility of the leader. The more it is spread around, the more effective it becomes if done properly. When it moves into the broader arena, it takes the form of public relations. All persons involved in ARE, including the adult learners, should be encouraged to sponsor ARE with expressions of honest enthusiasm. In the human condition, word of mouth testimony outweighs reports. Several parishioners who mention to the pastor and parish council president how much they value a program will have an impact. However, the image created by brochures, reports, news releases, etc., cannot be underplayed. Professional, eye-catching, straightforward print media also make lasting impressions of a successful operation. Seldom is public relations taught in ministerial training of any sort, but it should be. The wise leader or candidate finds a way to fill in the gap.

Networking or collaboration is being praised by most modern management specialists such as John Naisbitt, Peter Drucker, and Tom Peters. It also makes good sense for the Church. Rather than always doing their own thing, offices would work jointly in planning, delivering, and evaluating a program project. The procedure usually increases participation and revenue, cuts costs, and establishes a respect, knowledge, and trust in working relationships. In true collaborative efforts, there is a payoff for all units involved. It is the way of the future, but leaders must be prepared to be different kinds of managers involved in the intricacies of human resource development. Leaders must recognize that their best investment is the time they spend with the people they manage or work with. They must strive to facilitate and enable the strengths of others and not simply their own. Enabling is not an alien concept to the leaders in ARE, for it has been their responsibility in working with the learner as David pointed out in his paper. However, it is harder to apply in the relationship with peers or staffs, especially where there has been a keen sense of competition.

The need for ARE integration and recognition into the church structures and systems is not simply for its own benefit. What it brings in its methodologies, philosophy, and experience would enrich the ministerial work of every office serving adults. Perhaps through integration, the great discovery of ARE will happen!

Where collaboration has not been an established practice, it may be looked upon with suspicion. Peter F. Drucker, in his latest book, *Innovation and Entrepreneurship* makes the point that "Most innovations in public service institutions (including churches) are imposed on them either by outsiders or by catastrophe."[1] I don't see the shortage of vocations to the priesthood in that category. It could be a crisis, but it need not be, and it may be the leverage to open up collaboration between the clergy and laity. The teaching role of the priest is one of his most vital reponsibilities. Most of his teaching is directed to adults. It would seem that collaboration between the priest and the ARE leader would be natural. Most often it hasn't been, but there are many hope-filled signs. The studies of the ARE leader should include the partnership of priest and leader when they are focusing on human resource development and relationships. Priests who had the opportunity to study adult education have found a wealth of insights they continually draw upon in parish situations beyond their teaching role as well as in it.

Quality control is more than evaluation. It is a proactive use of a set of standards, established by each profession, that sees the product of program through from inception to delivery. The results are more likely to be high level and effective. As yet, a firm set of standards has not been instituted for ARE, although I see criteria for it evolving from the use of the ARE guidelines of needs assessment, planning, implementation, evaluation, and the substeps which are part of each.

Quality control provides the leader with a self-monitoring performance review as well as a means of accountability for all persons who work on the program. The leader can ill afford to overlook a program being designed in a vacuum or the actions of a short-tempered registrar while demanding detailed prepping of the presenter.

---

[1]Peter F. Drucker, *Innovation and Entrepreneurship—Practice and Principles* (New York: Harper and Row, 1985), p. 177.

The topic given the presenter, no matter how expertly delivered, could be of little interest to the potential learners, and the lack of courtesy could turn off interest for considerable time. Quality control doesn't allow for lapses. Tom Peter says in *Passion for Excellence* that all involved must "live the quality message with passion, persistence, and above all, consistency."[2]

I wish to clarify that a set of standards does not cause planning or design to be static or rigid. Creativity and flexibility are constitutive to quality control. So is the need for continuous learning and relearning on the part of the leader. Creativity and continuous learning lead us into the future and the leader's role as entrepreneur.

In the 1960s, ARE leaders were by necessity, to one degree or another, entrepreneurs who assumed risks for the sake of results. Risks lessened as patterns emerged. As we move into a predictably changing period in human history, the ARE leader should take on that role again. The leader should be open and outward-looking to satisfy the changing needs of the learner, whether they are in literacy, management of change, marital counseling, or religious subjects. D. Randy Garrison predicts that, "Future delivery structures must reflect the concept of an open learning system. . . . a system which is very much learner-centered and makes use of both traditional classroom and societal settings, as well as using a variety of methods that may not be technologically based."[3]

Technology poses a new learning challenge to the ARE: how to acquire a knowledge of it and adapt it without violating the human element which has been a core benefit in the learning process. In Naisbett's "High Tech/High Touch" society, the personal cannot be eliminated. High priority must be given to quality interaction with the teacher and content, and the curriculum design be sensitive and respectful to cultural differences. These cannot be overlooked in the scramble to make the message of the Church easily available.

Conclusion

Both David's article and my response can be applied to all ministries within the Church. We each seek to have readers see their leadership in a larger perspective. While the theological and administrative mating may seem like a strange marriage, looking at the reality of Church

---

[2]Tom Peters and Nancy Austin, *A Passion for Excellence* (New York: Random House, 1985) p. 99.

[3]D. Randy Garrison, "The Role of Technology in Continuing Education," *Continuing Education in the Year 2000* (Winter 1987): 36, p. 49, Ralph G. Brockett, Editor, New Directions for Continuing Education, (San Francisco: Jossey-Bass, Inc. No. 36, Winter 1987) p. 49.

and society today and sensing tomorrow, I believe it will provide a stable union. However, no degree of theological or administrative skill will make the leaders effective without a personal commitment to the person of Jesus Christ and an awareness and recognition of the Spirit moving within the community of faith.

Suggested Readings

McBrien, Richard P., *Ministry—A Theological, Pastoral Handbook* (New York: Harper and Row, 1987).

Naisbitt, John and Aburdence, Patricia, *Re-inventing the Corporation* (New York: Warner Books, 1985).

Schon, Donald A. *Educating the Reflective* Practitioner (San Francisco: Jossey-Bass, Inc., Publishers, 1987).

Whitehead, James D. and Evelyn Eaton, *Method in Ministry* (New York: Seabury Press, 1987).

Theological Perspectives on Adult Religious Education

John L. Elias

My question in this article is a simple one: Is there any value to reflecting theologically on adult learning, especially that which takes place in a religious context? Would a theologian from a particular tradition, drawing on theological sources and themes, have anything to offer adult educators? This will be my inquiry. My basic feeling is that theological reflection adds to our understanding of every human activity. But how this works out in practice is the thrust of this inquiry.

Insofar as religious persons reflect on their lives of faith, they are beginning theologians. Reflection on the life of faith is at the heart of the theological enterprise. Those who educate themselves in theology and those who are trained in it depend on their religious and spiritual lives, their lives of faith, to do theology. Without a personal and communal life of faith, one cannot truly be involved in theological enterprise.

I say this from the perspective of the Roman Catholic tradition. I am sure that what I say has some applicability beyond this context, but I do not intend to develop this. It may be the particularities of religious faith that best bring out the theological perspectives on adult learning. Yet one must also be aware that taking a particular perspective may lead to making claims that appear to be universal and which do not do justice to other religious faiths.

Faith as a Process of Learning

Faith is many things in the Christian tradition. In Dulles' analysis (1977) there is a threefold meaning of faith. Faith is *knowing* about God and the meaning of human existence. Secondly, faith is *trusting* in God as our protector, savior, and redeemer. Finally, faith is *acting* according to our beliefs. In this analysis, the first form of faith has been emphasized in the Roman Catholic tradition, the second is stressed in the churches of the Protestant reformation, and the third has received special attention in recent years from political and liberation theologians.

In each of these aspects of Christian faith, it is clear that learning is involved. To *know about God* and human existence entails learning. Paul makes the case that believing entails that someone learns, that someone is preached to (Romans 14ff). One way in which one grows in faith is by learning more about the life of faith: prayer, worship, witness, and service. One can learn more about God in various ways: silence, reflection, meditation, reading, study, sharing with and listening to others, and contemplation. All of these modes have their place in the lives of believers.

Growing in faith through increased knowledge is needed throughout life. The learning process begins in childhood when the rudiments of faith and basic attitudes are learned from parents. As a person grows older, formal education in churches supplements and deepens this knowledge. Learning about religious matters should ideally continue throughout life for the simple reason that faith can shed light on new and complex human experiences. It has been shown that persons have a need to reformulate or renegotiate their images of God throughout the life span (Rizzutto, 1979). A child's or adolescent's knowledge of God is not adequate to the developmental crises experienced in adulthood.

Faith as *trust in God* also demands learning throughout life. In the Protestant tradition this learning is primarily biblical knowledge as applied to one's life experience. At the basis of faith as trust is a knowledge of what God has done for the people of Israel and the followers of Jesus. God's fidelity is manifested in great deeds of salvation and promises of salvation. Our trust is based on these deeds and promises recorded in the Scriptures. They give us a surety that God is still acting in this manner towards us today and that the promises of God and Jesus extend to us.

While religious trust begins in infancy through our primary relationships, it demands a learning that continues throughout life. There are many situations wherein as adults we are tempted to abandon trust, to mistrust, or distrust the fidelity and promises of God. Illness, accidents, death of loved ones, loss of jobs, depressions, disillusionments, and other human experiences can severely test our trust in God. In these situations we need a confidence that can in part be supplied by a deepened learning about God's promises and ways. We can turn again to the Scriptures and find events, stories, prayers, and words that restore our faith as trust. We can look to the witness of other Christians who have undergone similar experiences. Relearning, new learning, additional learning can thus lead to a life of deepened trust in God.

Faith as action presupposes a learning. In some cases, the Christian response is clear: prayer, worship, witness, and service. But the call for Christians to live their faith in the world, in political, social, economic, and cultural spheres, is not a simple matter. This challenge demands a knowledge that comes through learning to translate the principles of the Gospels to the multiple spheres in which we live. A study of the two pastorals of the American bishops, one on peace and war and the other on the economy, shows how complex is the translation from Gospel and theology to practical steps of action. Not only must one know the Gospel, one must also know about many aspects of human life and endeavor.

Adults are in the best position to bring faith and gospel values into all areas of human life. They have the knowledge and the power to influence the direction of social and political change in society. To do this, however, a twofold learning must take place. They must learn increasingly about the Christian tradition and how it has grappled in the past with social, political, economic, and cultural issues. At the same time, they must assess changing realities in these areas before undertaking suitable action. Even so, it must be recognized that Christians do not always reach the same conclusions on either what the Gospel means or on what it demands in particular situations.

Learning in the Community of Faith

Thus far, I have considered learning in faith principally as an individual activity. I shall now consider adult learning from the perspective of the church or community of faith. The Christian church at both local and broader levels is a learning community. What the churches learn is more than what individuals learn. As churches develop, grow, face problems, and make decisions, they go through learning processes. Thus, the very nature of a church or community of faith entails a group of people who learn in order to keep their faith alive.

In the Christian church, this continued learning is called *tradition*. Tradition is a process by which truths, beliefs, and ways of life are received by a community, enriched by its life, and then handed on to new members. The Christian Scriptures developed at a particular moment in the tradition and history of the Church. While they are fundamental, a full understanding of Christian life entails knowledge of how those Scriptures were lived, interpreted, argued about, extended, and applied at particular times. Christian learning after biblical times is manifest in the writings of the fathers of the Church, the decrees of the great councils, the speculations of theologians and mystics, the writings of the reformers, and contemporary church teaching. Christian tradition is a sign of a living and learning group of people who look to past teachings but who also use all available human resources to fathom the meaning of Christian faith and its application to the problems and issues of today.

Within the tradition and learning of the Church, there has always been room for what is called *sensus fidelium* (the sense of the faithful). Persons who faithfully live the Christian life have valid understandings and interpretations of Christian faith. It is especially important to listen to the faithful in matters where they have special competence.

35

The sense of the faithful contributes to the tradition's being a living and learning process. It also contributes to the Church's being a learning community, because of its willingness to listen to the voices of its members. Since theology has developed in the Christian churches as principally a clerical and professional enterprise, it is important to listen to voices of nonclerics and laypersons.

A corollary of the first two points is that equal emphasis should be placed on *the learning Church* and the *teaching Church*. Authentic teachers are those who have learned and continue to learn. Only a Church of faith that constantly engages in learning can teach with authority. The learning Church is one that will be listened to and heeded. A community may teach, but the effectiveness of its teaching is conditioned by how well the members accept and learn from it.

If we believe survey polls, there have been some teachings in recent years that have not received widespread acceptance. One can interpret this in various ways. Authorities may presume that nonacceptance indicates that more strenuous and effective efforts must be made to ensure that the teachings are better understood and accepted. On the other hand, a teaching may not be accepted because the teachers are ill prepared; they have not opened themselves up to all sources of knowledge on the issue. Which of these interpretations is correct will have to be examined case by case.

Within the Christian community there are many teachers and many learners. There are also teachings that are presented with various degrees of authoritativeness. The process of learning and discernment is a continuing one in which all can participate. Individual thought and freedom are to be respected. But weight must also be given to the learning that comes from authority and tradition. While there is a certain presumption given to authority and tradition, the freedom and responsibility of individuals to learn, discern, and come to judgments are of high value in the community of faith.

Modes of Adult Learning in the Churches

Before looking at particular modes of religious learning, I will first point out a major difference in Christian understanding of faith and learning. In some Christian communities, faith and learning are viewed as the activities of God within us. The emphasis is placed on God's activity. Augustine explained knowing as divine illumination. In this viewpoint, faith is a gift of God—God's presence within us, God seeking us and instructing us interiorly. What we must do is merely open ourselves to this influence from God and we will believe and learn what we need to know.

Another type of Christian theology emphasizes Christian faith and learning as our personal search for God and the meaning of human existence. The emphasis here is on our activity of seeking, searching, learning, listening, studying. While not denying God's role in these processes, what is stressed is human efforts at understanding and arriving at wisdom and faith. While the first form of theology takes a mystical view of our relationship to God, this second viewpoint emphasizes the human effort.

In our life of faith, we can see both of these positions as having validity. There are times when we feel acted upon, passive, recipients of God's action. Our faith and understandings appear as gifts from beyond and not the result of our own efforts. At other times, we know that we have painfully searched and learned and come to understanding. At least this is how we interpret what is happening within us.

Recognizing this unresolvable tension in theology and spirituality we can look at a number of modes of religious learning in order to understand their dynamics.

One mode is that of *silence*. My experience with British Quakers convinced me of the value of learning through silence. To sit with a group of Christians from thirty minutes to an hour is to learn about God, myself, and others. An inner light illumines us. God does not need silence, but we do. When silence becomes the chief mode of reflection and union with God, as it is with Quakers, we realize its value. It is good to think our own thoughts which we then come to recognize as God's thoughts. It is almost anticlimactic when someone at the Quaker meeting begins to share reflections with others. Still, there is a value to this personal sharing. I found myself on one occasion giving voice to deep feelings which I had barely recognized within me.

An ancient mode of Christian prayer and learning is the slow and meditative reading of the Scriptures, the *lectio divina*. This form of religious learning depends on reading little but pondering it deeply. The basic attitude of the Christian learner in this mode is to listen to God speaking through the words and events of the Scriptures. This individual activity fills one with images from the tradition. The passages take on new meaning, not so much in themselves, but because of our changed situation. The events and words come alive because they are intertwined with our own events and words. The words challenge how we live; they present a way of life for us. The events and words of our experience search the Scriptures for meaning and understanding.

Though it may appear odd to some, *prayer* can be viewed as a mode of learning. I have learned through prayer, not so much the formal prayers which are memorized and recited—though one should not ignore what we have learned through them—but the prayer that is mental, meditative, or contemplative. We do not pray in order to

37

learn; learning is not given as one of the ends or purposes of prayer. But learning is often part of the process or at least a by-product. Through lifting mind and heart to God, we learn about God, ourselves, others, failings, successes, fears, and joys. The learning that comes through prayer is not informational; it is rather attitudinal or value-oriented. It is this type of learning that changes us and enriches our lives.

Formal *Christian worship* is a mode of learning. Adults gather together not just to worship God but to learn about God and about what God is doing in their lives and in the world. There are so many ways in which Christian worship is a learning experience. We learn through song, readings, prayers, architecture, preaching, and such intangibles as climate and atmosphere. Much of the learning is often a reinforcement of what we already know and adhere to. But on occasion we are startled into thinking about things differently—God, self, world, relationships to others.

A danger of formalized worship for learning is that we may become too comfortable with it, thus failing to see it with fresh eyes. But there can also be surprise moments, moments of grace and understanding.

Thus far in my discussion of modes of adult learning in the Church, I have focused on the learning of individuals. Even worship was viewed insofar as individuals learn by participation in liturgical experiences of the Church. Now I would like to look at a number of modes of adult learning where group experiences are paramount.

There is a long tradition in the Church of *small group learning*. The first example of this may have been the gathering of the disciples with Mary awaiting the coming of the Spirit. A belief that the small group has a primacy in prayer, learning, and faith sharing goes back to the words of Jesus: "For where two or three are gathered in my name, there am I in the midst of them" (Matthew 18:20).

There have been many forms of small group gatherings to penetrate the meaning of Christian faith and to offer mutual support in living out the demands of the Gospel. In the monastic movement, love of God and love of learning were beautifully combined. Medieval schools, brotherhoods, and sisterhoods were manifestations of this desire to combine fellowship, prayer, and learning. The churches of the reform, especially the Methodists and Puritans, made extensive use of small gatherings. It has been argued that the origin of the modern small group movement began with Protestants who believed that the Spirit of God was more likely to inspire small gatherings of Christians (Oden, 1972). One of the earliest examples of adult education in this country were the groups of Puritans who met under the supervision of great pastors like Cotton Mather.

There are many other examples of small Christian groups in which fellowship, prayer, and learning have a place. The most recent examples within Roman Catholicism are the basic Christian communities in Latin America and elsewhere. In these small gatherings, people reflect on the meaning of the Gospel in their lives, especially as it pertains to social, political, economic, and cultural structures. These communities are not all of one kind, but they are all based on the fundamental nature of the Christian church as a community of disciples who believe that the Spirit of God comes through group fellowship, prayer, sharing, and action.

Another example of Christian adult learning takes place in more formal gatherings in such events as *conferences, synods, and councils*. All Christian churches have one form or another of these structures in order to deliberate on the meaning of the Gospel for contemporary issues. While in England, I followed carefully the annual Anglican Synods in which deliberations took place on the ordination of women and the doctrinal position of Anglicanism on such issues as the divinity of Jesus, the virgin birth, and the resurrection of Jesus. The Anglican Church in New Jersey has been grappling for the past few years with issues in sexual morality. In these gatherings, while the ultimate aim is to issue a teaching, the entire process is one of learning and discernment.

Within my own Roman Catholic church I have witnessed in my lifetime dramatic events of deliberation and learning with a view to teaching. The Second Vatican Council, which has shaped my thinking for two decades, was a worldwide learning experience. No one could have predicted the final documents and the positions taken, even though a small group of Vatican bureaucrats seemed to have thought their preliminary drafts would carry the day. Those bishops who intervened early and called for the rejection of the drafts were saying that we need to learn more, we need to listen to the many voices of experience and to professional theologians.

Closer to home, we have had the recent experience of the American bishops' use of elaborate consultative processes in order that they might learn what to teach on peace and war and on the American economy. It is significant that they were open to learn from theologians, philosophers, social scientists, economists, politicians, and ordinary persons. We have all benefited from their long and extensive learning, which shaped what they taught. In so learning and then teaching, they have continued a long Christian tradition whereby we appeal to the gathering of Christians in order to learn to resolve our differences.

These modes of learning, both individual, small group, and institutional, are based on long-standing theologies of Christian communities, their traditions, and their discernments. There are obvious tensions among these various modes. Different churches give priority to one or more over others. Some of the fundamental differences that divide Christians are found in these modes of Christian learning and the results of the learning processes. But the fundamental theological principles are clear. Christians learn as individuals, in groups, and through institutional efforts. God is an integral part of this learning process. This does not mean that individual modes will not clash with group and institutional modes. Any reading of Christian history shows the potential for conflict.

Is there, perhaps, a still deeper theological reason and explanation for the critical importance for Christian adults to engage in lifelong learning about their faith? I think there is. A fundamental reason for continued learning is that Jesus, whom we worship, through whose power we learn, was himself, a learner.

Theologians have grappled for years with the different types of knowledge that Jesus possessed in his divine and human natures. The Christian Scriptures certainly present him as a person who learned, who was surprised and often disappointed in what he learned.

In the story about the young Jesus in the temple, he is presented as both teaching and asking questions of those learned in the Jewish religion. Though I've usually thought of his questioning as a form of finding out what the learned temple dwellers knew, he could very well have been trying to learn from them.

Conclusion

For me there is a certain unity about the various adult learnings I have explored in this paper. I realize that I could have developed other theological themes such as revelation and salvation and related them to adult learning. But the themes I have chosen are essential themes. Simply put, my point is that learning is a reality in human life that is integral to all persons, groups, and institutions. It is integral to Christian individuals, groups, and institutions. The process of learning is one in which God participates in a way that is appropriate to divinity. Jesus was a learner in his earthly existence. The Christian churches throughout their history have learned and relearned many things. Groups of Christians have met in the past and are meeting today in religious settings in which learning is a part. Individual Christians grow in faith by learning more about God, themselves, the world in which they live, and the teaching of their religious bodies.

Perhaps one of our problems with adult learning is a deeply theological one. We often hear about adults not growing in the faith, not learning more about their faith as they progress through the adult life cycle. Though this failure may be explained by social scientists and researchers, perhaps part of the explanation is theological. A theology of nonlearning may be a partial explanation for this failure. Concepts of an omniscient and unlearning Jesus and an infallible and unlearning church may subtly influence adults to be unlearning Christians. (Hull, 1986)

In this article, I have presented a particular theological viewpoint. It puts growth, process and learning at the heart of human and divine existence. I find this perspective helpful to me as I try to understand myself, my Christian faith, my Church, and most importantly my relationship to God. I hope this perspective may do something of the same for you.

References

Dulles, Avery, "The Meaning of Faith Considered in Relationship to Justice," in J. Haughey, Editor, *The Faith That Does Justice* (Ramsey, New Jersey: Paulist Press, 1977).

Hull, John, *What Prevents Christian Adults from Learning?* (London: SCM Press, 1986).

LeClerq, J., *Love of God and Love of Learning* (New York: Fordham University Press, 1948).

Oden, Thomas, *The Intensive Group Experience: The New Pietism* (Philadelphia: The Westminster Press, 1972).

Rizzutto, Ana-Maria, *The Birth of the Living God* (Chicago: University of Chicago Press, 1979).

Thorndike, Edward, *Adult Learning* (New York: Macmillan Publishing Company, 1928).

A Church That Learns: A Response to Theological Perspectives on Adult Religious Education

John R. Zaums

As I read John Elias' article, a scene from my past came to mind. A few years ago, while stuck in a traffic jam, I caught sight of a bumper sticker that probably most of us have seen. It read, "Jesus is the Answer!" I can still picture myself fighting the irrational temptation to roll down the window and shout at the car, "But, what's the question?" For I knew that no matter how often we're exposed to *answers*, religious or otherwise, little or no learning takes place without prior questioning, reflection, and frequently, dialogue.

Elias observes that the Scriptures present Jesus as a learner. A reflective reading of the Gospels reveals that Jesus appears to have learned in many ways—alone and with others, in silence and in dialogue, in prayer and in action, through questioning and listening. It is upon the latter two that I'd like to initially focus my reflections.

The first picture we have of Jesus following the infancy narratives shows him asking questions of the temple officials. He retained this penchant for questioning throughout his life. In fact, the Scriptures record 154 questions asked by Jesus, both of others and of himself. Instead of responding with answers, Jesus constantly forced questioners back on their own resources, often by *answering* them with other questions. In doing so he challenged them, as Elias comments, to *theologize*, i.e., to reflect upon their tradition and to search out truth in light of their own lived experience of faith.

I think, however, it is significant to note that in his desire to learn through questioning, Jesus not only addressed and listened to religious officials; he also questioned and learned from a diverse group of individuals, including both Jew and Samaritan, priest and soldier, leper and parent. I believe, and I think Elias would concur, that there is a profound lesson here not only for each of us but also for the entire Church. Like Jesus, every Christian, as well as the Church itself, should raise questions, and should listen to and reflect upon the *sensus fidelium*, upon the understanding and interpretation that faithful Christians bring to these questions. As Elias notes, one of the ways in which the Catholic Church in America is attempting to follow the example of Jesus in this regard is by utilizing a consultative process in developing perspectives on issues of peace, the economy, and women. I firmly agree with Elias that a church that learns in such a consultative fashion will be better listened to and heeded because it has *touched base*; it has questioned and listened to various groups and has tapped diverse sources of knowledge.

But while questioning and listening to others, we need to realize, as Elias points out, that churches as well as sincere Christians do not always come to the same conclusions "both on interpretations of what the Gospel means and of what it demands in particular situations." Such a realization raises a perennial question which I'd like to reflect upon during the remainder of my response. The question is this: While listening, how can the Church as a community of believers remain faithful to its tradition and, at the same time, sincerely respect and learn from those believers, both within and outside of the Church, who hold differing perspectives?

For the Catholic Church to remain both faithful and willing to learn from differing voices and sometimes clashing perspectives requires a theology of Church solidly grounded in the documents of Vatican II. The Pilgrim Church proclaimed by Vatican II does not profess to have a monopoly on all possible truth, and the truth that it possesses remains incomplete. Because the Church is a pilgrim, it has to be constantly on the move. The law of its present existence is a law of development, a law of growth and continual reformation. The truth which the Church today proclaims must always stand under scrutiny, remain open to new perspectives, and be subject to debate so that a richer truth can emerge. This dynamic nature of truth is affirmed in the *Declaration on Religious Freedom:*

> Truth, however, is to be sought after in a manner proper to the dignity of the person and his social nature. The inquiry is to be free, carried on with the aid of teaching or instruction, communication, and dialogue. In the course of these, men explain to one another the truth they have discovered, or think they have discovered, in order to thus assist one another in the quest for truth. Moreover, as the truth is discovered, it is by a personal assent that men are to adhere to it (Abbott, *Documents of Vatican II*, pp. 680–681).

Thus, divergent positions discussed in honest and open dialogue should incite and challenge the Church not only to rethink and reword but to purify and further develop the truth which it partially apprehends and humbly proclaims. In doing so, however, it must be stressed that the Church can never *give up* what it knows through faith to be essential for some other *truth*. The Church is involved in a quest, a search, for expanded truth, deeper truth, but not different truth.

Thus, the Church is a pilgrim in regard to its developing perception of truth concerning itself, the world, ourselves, and God. Or stated differently in light of Elias' article, the theology of a learning Church is a developing theology. Ever since John Henry Newman's *Essay on the Development of Christian Doctrine* appeared, theologians have attempted to define exactly what he meant by dogmatic development. The paradox of having and not yet having the truth was clearly understood by Newman. For him, the fullness of all truth has been revealed once and for all in the person of Jesus. However, the Church's understanding of Jesus, the ultimate revelation, is still in process. Theological development results from our continuing attempt to understand more clearly and to express more accurately for today the Gospel that lives in the Church's memory. As the Church questions, listens, and learns, revelation takes on new perspectives and dimensions. But this development does not change the divine reality nor do true beliefs suddenly become false. What does happen, however, is that in shifting the focus of inquiry and in expressing a belief differently, something new can be learned and stated that wasn't explicitly noticed before.

In our individual quest for truth, each of us, like the Church itself, must neither give up our claim to truth, nor too rigidly hold to our every position as lasting and definite. As faithful persons, we are called upon to humbly proclaim and act upon our best perception of truth. But at the same time, as learners in the faith, we are called upon, while refraining from proclaiming the finality of our perceptions, to listen to, respect, and learn from the perceptions held by others.

To be faithful yet, at the same time, to be open—this I believe is one of the key challenges that Elias' thought presents to both the learning Christian and the learning Church. In *Becoming Adult, Becoming Christian,* James Fowler contends that only the mature adult who lives a life reflective of a higher stage of faith development is capable of meeting such a challenge. At this stage which Fowler calls "conjunctive faith," truth is seen as rich, multiform, ambiguous, and complex. Conjunctive faith combines a deep commitment to one's own tradition with, first, a genuine and humble openness to often contradictory perspectives held by differing traditions and communities and, second, a recognition that the quest for truth often requires a dialectical interplay of such perspectives (pp. 65–67). If Fowler is correct in assuming that the qualities of faithfulness and openness are indicative of a higher stage of faith development, it necessarily follows that, for the learning Church to be truly faithful and open, it must increasingly become a community of mature adult Christians, a community which is challenged and challenges each of its members to grow in faith and to learn as Jesus learned —whether alone or with others, in silent seeking or in dialogue, in prayer or in action.

From the many possible insights presented by Elias, I have chosen to focus on only those few that most profoundly spoke to me, and that personally challenged me to question and to reflect. I found the concepts of a Jesus who learned and of a Church that learns particularly revealing and thus much of what I've attempted to develop here relates to both concepts. While reading Elias' article you may find yourself focusing upon other ideas which speak more directly to you. My hope is that your reflections upon his insights will be as revealing for you as mine personally have been.

44

Unity and Diversity within Adult Religious Education

C. Michael Lebrato

I. Introduction

As I watched the television coverage of the pope's visit this past September, I was struck by the great variety of people who took part in the many events. They were Hispanic, White, Black, Asian, and Native American; they were female and male, young and old, sick and well.

As the pope met with this rich mixture of people, he heard different concerns, needs, and thoughts expressed about being Catholic in the United States today. Some speakers were apparently quite comfortable with the way things are in the Church; others strongly advocated for major changes. Some affirmed the pope's leadership style; others asked to have it altered. Some advocated for their special concerns; others presented global priorities. Clearly, not all were in agreement with one another, nor with the pope.

Yet whatever we might say about the pope's visit, his views and his leadership style, he symbolizes to us Catholics a profound unity of faith and religion which we share with one another. The differences which we experienced during his visit at times became secondary to the strong feelings of pride and unity at being Roman Catholic engendered by the presence of John Paul II. He is our POPE. And as *our* pope, he is not simply an abstract symbol of the official magisterial Church. He is a concrete, living expression of the religious unity that all of us, from the most conservative to the most liberal, have in common.

The papal visit, in all of its dimensions, became a sort of microcosm of who we are as Church in this country. We are a people highly diverse in both our backgrounds and experiences of life and in our religious beliefs and practices; yet we remain deeply unified in our religion and our faith.

As we look to the decade of the 90s, we are challenged to give serious attention to unity and diversity within the Church. Since the Second Vatican Council, a number of tensions in the Church have jelled around this issue. While many of us have welcomed the greater pluralism and diversity within the Church made possible by the Council, others have seen these developments as a threat to church unity. At the heart of these tensions are different understandings of the nature of the Church.

How these often conflicting perspectives impact adult religious education is the topic of this paper. But before turning our attention to the

45

contemporary aspects of unity and diversity, it would do well to first consider some of the historical dimensions of the issue.

II. Unity and Diversity within the Church

A. The Early Church and Scripture

The issue of unity and diversity is as old as the Church itself. The New Testament, for example, is rich in its varied interpretations of Jesus. He is presented to us as the Messiah, the new Moses, the Savior, the miracle worker; as priest, as prophet, and as king. In its gradual refinement of the oral traditions that were later gathered into the New Testament, the Church decided to hold onto these various perspectives because they each added some important dimension to our understanding of Jesus.

Likewise, when the Church debated over what was to comprise its canon of Scripture, it recognized that no single Gospel was sufficient to adequately express who Jesus was. So, even at the risk of including some conflicting information about him, the Church embraced four different Gospels of Jesus. And, well that it did, because the diverse perspectives of Jesus that we find in the four Gospels give us a much greater insight into his life and mission. For example, in John, Jesus is the eternal Son of God; Matthew presents him as the promised Messiah, son of Abraham, son of David; Mark sees Jesus as savior and healer of humankind; and Luke heralds him as the fulfillment of the Law, of the Old Testament promises of God.

Each Gospel adds a more complete revelation of the person of Jesus. Thus, the Church has even within its foundational Scripture, its most sacred writings, a rich diversity that illuminates both its own identity and that of Jesus, its founder.

B. The Diversity of Early Christian Life

Pentecost symbolized the far-ranging diversity that was to eventually characterize the Christian Church. "Devout Jews of every nation under heaven" (Acts 2:5) gathered around Peter and the other apostles to hear the Good News proclaimed.

Breaking away from its sectarian identity within Judaism, the Church quickly became more universal, expanding in its rituals, theologies, and spiritualities. This growing diversity helped give the Church a vitality and adaptability that enabled it to attract converts from many different populations and cultures. Had the Church curtailed diversification or solidified into a singular religious expression, it is unlikely that it would have been able to achieve its present identity of being at home in all places and cultures.

It is this rich diversity that gave birth to so many of our present forms of Christian life and spirituality. Thus, we have a wide spectrum of formal religious communities with different ways of life, e.g., Franciscan, Augustinian, Dominican, Carmelite. This diversity is even more pronounced in lay life and movements. There is the Apostolate of the Laity, the Christian Family Movement, Marriage Encounter, Cursillo, Charismatic renewal, Opus Dei, Eastern and Western forms of piety, to name but a few.

While the Church was diversifying, it was also taking steps to preserve the unity of its faith. Its rapid growth and adaptation to local circumstances required it to develop more integrated structures and a stronger, centralized teaching authority. Also, each time a major controversy arose, the Church clarified its thinking on the issue, thereby adding to its growing body of teachings and regulations.

These developments helped preserve a unified faith, though not always without negative consequences. The struggle to preserve unity often produced unnecessary uniformity. Thus, there eventually arose for many areas of the world, the requirement for one ritual language, one way of celebrating the sacred rites, one way of understanding the sacred mysteries. By the time of the Second Vatican Council, the Church had lost some of the beauty and power of its own inherent diversity.

C. Vatican II: Liturgy, Theology, and Ecumenism

By the time the Second Vatican Council completed its work, the Church was enthusiastically rediscovering its past diversity. The beauty and depth of the Oriental, Asian, African, and Arabian Churches and their experiences of our common faith were, once again, being recognized and appreciated.

In the wake of renewal of Vatican II, we are becoming an ever more catholic church, universal in our embrace of people and of their experiences of the divine life. The liturgical renewal in the Church, which continues even today, is richer because of the exchange of worship experienced between the east and west, north and south, and between the various Christian traditions both within and outside the Catholic Church.

Likewise, Vatican II precipitated a resurgence of theological investigation that has led to expanding understandings and perspectives of the mysteries of our faith. While at times we may struggle with the diversity of these theologies, we nevertheless have become a more credible and viable witness of the Gospel to the world.

It is especially encouraging to see the progress in ecumenism begun by Vatican II when, for the first time in hundreds of years, we recognize the life and activity of the Spirit in other Christian religions, and non-Christian religions. This recognition of the diversity of God's activity in the world's religious traditions gives great hope that we can and will be united under the one divine "Father of us all."

D. Unity and Diversity Today

While many may see the hallmark of unity within the Catholic Church in terms of uniformity, in fact, diversity is essential to its life and mission. Indeed, there may have been times when the Church had underemphasized its diversity or had sought to diminish it. But, there is no real unity without diversity. These are two sides of the same coin. Unity without diversity is narrow sectarianism. And diversity without unity is useless relativism. Both *unity in diversity* and *diversity in unity* are needed for the Church to have a healthy, vibrant, and stable faith life.

The challenge for us in the Church today is one of degree and balance. The resolution of this issue does not depend upon which side of the dichotomy to come down on but rather upon how we honor both the unity that ties us together as well as the diversity that identifies our uniqueness. How specifically can we define our unity without sacrificing our diversity? And how universally can we embrace diversity without destroying our unity?

III. Why an Issue in the 90s for Adult Religious Educators?

Unity and Diversity surfaces as an *issue* for adult religious educators facing the 90s in at least three aspects of our ministry: in the makeup of the Church in America, in the complexities of contemporary life, and in our role as educators in the Church today.

A. Make Up of the Church in America

Unity and Diversity is an issue of great importance for the 90s if for no other reason than that the face of America is changing. We have always been a highly diverse culture or, more correctly, a collection of cultures. But, in recent times, we have been experiencing a new influx of immigrants who are altering the ways in which we are a society and a Church.

In the past, we tended to think of ourselves as a Church with European roots—Irish, Polish, Italian, French, etc. But now, due to the changing profile of our population, this self-concept—though never really appropriate—is quickly changing. Most statistical projections show that the Church in America, which is already heavily Hispanic, may have a majority of Hispanics in the early years of the next century. How do we prepare for this change in our identity and in our ways of being Church? What are its implications for us as adult religious educators?

48

While Hispanics may be emerging as the single largest ethnic group in the Church, many other racial and ethnic populations in this country desire that their own ways be recognized and affirmed. Blacks, Native Americans, people from the Middle and Far East all deserve to see their religious experience somehow reflected in church life.

Other segments of the population that will influence the scope of our ministry include women and the elderly. The role of women in our society is expanding. Positions of influence which have traditionally been reserved for men are increasingly opened to women. The growing number of women theologians is providing us with a feminine perspective on faith and moral issues that hitherto had been unavailable. Women in positions of pastoral leadership are significantly contributing to the Church's increasing sensitivity to the needs of the poor and disenfranchised.

The elderly, who, until recently, were considered *unproductive*, are assuming more numerous roles of influence and leadership in society today. They are becoming a new and ever more utilized resource of volunteers in the Church to meet its growing ministerial demands.

Clearly, the demographics in our society are changing so radically that a majority of us now regularly meet, work, and worship with people whose backgrounds are quite diverse and varied from those of their own. Marriages and families of today are no longer characterized by a homogeneity which they once had, but instead, blend cultures, religions, value systems, psychosocial practices, and rituals.

The diversity of people with whom we live and work and worship presents a growing challenge to us as adult educators to open up the Gospels in new and varied ways. How can we, who may be part of the majority culture, effectively engage those who are from other cultures? How can we bring forward the wonderful riches of their traditions for the sake of learning by all? How can the feminine perspective be more effectively incorporated into the learning process, and how can the experience and wisdom of the elderly be tapped? Adult religious education in the coming years will need to be more varied in both content and design.

B. The Complexities of Contemporary Life

Today's life is complex. The simpler ways of the past are gone. Gone, too, are easy solutions to one-dimensional problems.

As we advance as a society, the fabric that makes up our lives is becoming more intricate and interwoven. For example, we can no longer simply speak of *the family;* we have nuclear families, single-parent families, reconstituted families, and so forth.

Our world is highly interdependent; activity in one area can and frequently does impact other areas. Consequently, our decisions have implications far beyond ourselves.

Technology is altering our lives at an increasing rate. Because of computers, our knowledge is expanding exponentially, thus making it increasingly difficult for someone to grasp fully a topic. We are becoming increasingly interdependent in our ability to address issues and solve problems.

Diversity is a natural consequence of the complexity of our times. Homogeneity is breaking down; we live different lives, with different issues, facing increasingly complex problems. It is becoming impossible for the Church to address all the problems and challenges that we face as Christians. Rather, the appropriate Christian response will necessarily have to surface from different sources, especially from among those who are dealing most directly with the issues.

This fact was evident in the processes used by the American hierarchy for developing pastorals on the topics of nuclear war and the economy. Faced with highly complex issues on each of those topics, the bishops had no choice but to consult both experts and laity about them.

Thus, as we attempt to apply the light of the Gospel to today's world, we see that we can no longer look exclusively to the Church's teaching office. Complexity has forced us to see truth as emanating from many persons and situations.

The process of adult religious education lends itself well to the growing complexity of our world and of our faith lives. In adult education, properly conceived, learners are also teachers. Each person has something to contribute, some grasp of truth that is important for others. Also, it is in the very heart of the learning experience that insights are often gained, breakthroughs made. In other words, the adult religious education process can be a forum where the challenges of contemporary life can be explored in the light of the Gospel. It is an appropriate place where the search for truth in the Spirit of Christ can take place.

As the 90s draw near, adult religious educators will be challenged to view their ministry not only as a way of *educating* the learners but also as a way of surfacing the education of the learners for the sake of the whole Church.

In our role as adult educators in the Church of the 90s, we must learn to blend the unity of the Gospel with the diversity of human life we experience in one another and in the increasingly complex situations in our world.

C. In Our Role as Educators in the Church Today

Prior to the Second Vatican Council, the dominant image of the Church was that of a monolithic structure where all the pieces fitted well together and where there was a sense of completeness. There was little internal disorder. The Church had a particular view of life and mission in which its members concurred. To be Catholic was to be part of a great unified religious experience that made good sense.

With the Second Vatican Council, that self-contained identity, that assurance of correctness and truth began to crumble. Our eyes were opened to new issues, new ways of seeing things. Where we had seen the Church only as a hierarchial structure, we now see it also as the people of God; where we had seen the world as essentially a place to retreat from, we now also see it as the place of God's redemptive activity; where we had seen other Christians as heretics and schismatics, we now see them as genuine communities of faith where the spirit of Jesus dwells.

Before the Second Vatican Council, we rejoiced in our unity, our oneness; following the Council, we rejoice in both our unity and our diversity. We now accept more diversity in practically every aspect of church life—in our doctrine, in our spirituality, in our sacramental life and rituals, and in our ways of responding to the gospel mandates. If the Second Vatican Council did anything, it allowed for the ineffable mystery of God in Jesus to be reflected, not simply through the one hierarchial voice, but through the many different voices which comprise the Church. In a sense, the multitude of talents and gifts with which God had endowed the Church were allowed to surface and to contribute to its overall identity and mission.

There now exists within the Church not simply one theology but many theologies, not simply one spirituality but a host of spiritualities. We now have not just one ritual, the Latin Mass, but a host of ways of celebrating the Lord's meal in language and cultural adaptation.

All of this places the adult religious educator in a very special position in the Church. The task of the educational process is to cultivate and affirm the rich diversity of experiences of Christian faith that exist within the Church without compromising the unity of faith. Adult educators help believers to interpret the Gospel for their lives while at the same time holding fast to the central beliefs of Christian life and practice.

Adult religious education classes will, by their very nature, bring together people who have diverse preferences in spirituality and ritual practice and different theological perspectives. This is simply the nature of today's Church. The challenge for the adult educator is not to merely manage these potentially conflicting viewpoints within the learning process, but to help the learners see the truth that abides in each of them. At the same time, the adult educator must serve as a credible witness on behalf of the Church and its teachings on the issues under discussion.

As practicing adult religious educators, we face two challenges.

First, how can we, with the passion that our work demands, present the teachings of the Church in their integrity and unity to the great diversity of people we serve? Secondly, how can we be effective ministers to adults who may, at times, experience those teachings as oppressive or even as contradictory to their own lived experiences?

These challenges exist for adult religious educators today because of the great diversity of experiences, disparate belief patterns, and thinking processes that people have. If adult Catholics were not to think for themselves, then it would be another matter. As it is, adults must reflect on their faith, ask questions of it, struggle with doubts about it, and make responsible moral decisions. If this is the kind of mature adult member the Church wants, then as adult educators we must learn to accept the ambiguities and tensions that will inevitably be part of our role.

IV. Conclusion

For us in adult education, the tension between unity and diversity is a healthy one. It is one which we not merely tolerate but cultivate. We recognize the value and importance of both unity and diversity.

But the challenge for us is to model in our own lives and in our work a blending of the unity and diversity of our Church in such a way that we are more effective ministers to discipleship.

How do we foster and serve the diverse qualities that enrich our church community that keep us growing and that enliven us by constantly creating us anew? How do we respect and encourage diversity within the Roman Catholic Church?

The temptation for us may be at times to come down on one side or the other of this dichotomy. But we must resist it. To do so would be to undermine the very ideals we stand for and to cripple the unique gift that adult religious education has for the Church.

Now, more than ever, we need to develop adult religious education in our parishes and communities, but always in a context of prayer and worship-rituals that bind us ever more intimately with the Spirit of God who is our source of unity. We are, all of us as Church, on a pilgrimage, a journey. We are in process. And, being in process, we are not without ambiguity, incompleteness, and even at times antagonistic factions.

How well we handle our new emerging diversity in the Church will bear heavily on how well we can bring the saving message of Jesus into the twenty-first century.

Reflections While Working Out at the YMCA: A Response to Unity and Diversity within Adult Religious Education

Alice M. Stefaniak

After reading "Unity and Diversity within the Catholic Church" (Lebrato), I went over to the Y where I work out several times a week. From the Y's balcony track you can view basketball, nautilus machines, volleyball, and aerobic exercises on the floor below. As I walked the track, I half-concentrated on the members of an aerobic exercise group who were working out with their instructor. They were a picture of unity and diversity, a varied array of exercise buffs who participated in different ways. Some were huffing and puffing; others were looking ecstatically high. Some were adapting creatively to directions; others were mimicking the instructor—all to one end: the health and well-being of their bodies and spirits.

They reminded me of some participants in a recent scripture class. Some were huffing and puffing after one night of scripture background; others were looking ecstatically high about new insights. Some were adapting creatively to the process; others were docilely mimicking the instructor—all to one end: the spiritual health and well-being of their minds and spirits.

I grinned when I thought about it: unity and diversity can be influenced very clearly, not only by the content, but also by the methods we use to work with people in adult education programs.

A few questions came to mind:

- Have we sufficiently explored different ways of getting learners actively involved, thereby promoting greater diversity?
- Do we tie together the elements of process and content so that by the end of the session, participants can see the unity of the theme we've pursued?
- Do we ask questions that allow people to think honestly and individually about the concepts, or do we create expectations for certain responses?
- Do we use processes that enable and encourage learners to explore the boundaries of their faith, or do we corral them into a kind of *frozen* Catholicism?
- Are we promoting both divergent thinking when the group needs

53

to explore an issue and convergent thinking when closure is needed?

When I arrived home, I remembered some adult education experiences that I had either attended or facilitated. The following are several concerns that I had.

1. Some people think that a lecture or a content-filled session automatically ensures unity among learners. But, the presentation on the content can—and frequently does—provoke all kinds of different reactions, including rebellion, if discussion or disagreement is not allowed. I think of this often at Sunday liturgies where week after week the participants only hear one person's view of the Word, effecting a kind of unity that unfortunately masks the Spirit's speaking in diverse models, tongues, and themes.

2. Many talented workshop speakers are seemingly oblivious to the participants' needs to reply, negate, create, discuss, exclaim, cogitate over, or go aside for a time. The speaker's behavior seems to suggest a belief that, during the workshop, adults are to stop thinking for themselves. They forget that *every moment* is time to construct consciously worldviews and to assess life values and beliefs.

Wonderfully intended workshops, conventions, and classes have been undermined by the notion that only one person can address the issue at a time, or that three discussion questions will take care of things. Creative ways of working with large and small groups need to be integrated into adult learning packages so as to enhance the diversity of the group. At the end of the experience, a facilitator can protect the unity that might have dissipated or appeared hidden through the process by tying loose ends together, strategizing the next steps, and forging a vision for the future.

3. Some people think that small group process is nothing more than a *sharing of ignorances,* and that people are not interested in such sharing; they only want the facts. From my experience, I am convinced that the fear that often surfaces regarding small groups is really a fear of the unknown rather than a genuine fear of *truth* getting lost in the process. If there is good facilitation, consensus decision making, a blend of opinion and reflection, and a consistent effort to build community, unity and diversity can be enriched together.

4. When groups try the dialogue model of education for the first time, the participants sometimes neglect to seek clarity and unity. In such cases, facilitators and group leaders need training in:

- learning how to narrow the focus after each person has sufficiently personalized the ideas,
- digging out the priority items from an intense brainstorming session,
- helping the group balance its obvious dices against the solid principles contained in religious systems and values,
- summarizing the group's positions and debating them,
- replaying the themes that surface repeatedly so that the group can check how representative they are of its views,
- guiding group members to examine their underlying assumptions so that they don't replace principles,
- having a clear vision of where the group is heading in each step of the process,
- comparing the insights of group members with their religious values,
- ending a session with reflection and clarifying questions to help group members deal constructively with their beliefs.

5. Some facilitators seemingly encourage diversity, but in the final analysis they are not really open to it. Although the *open* signs may be present, (e.g., discussion, time for reflection, open-ended questions) when the discussion touches practical application, questions authority, or challenges the structure, the facilitator closes down the process.

These are only five vignettes of adult education that come to mind. They represent areas where a clear understanding of the interrelationship between learning methods and the promotion of unity within diversity is important.

We know that worldviews are constantly changing as are our attitudes toward diversity and unity. In the early Church, diversity flowered until the charisms and gifts became too much for an established institutionalized religion to cope with. Then some unity of expression was enforced in ways of viewing God, the world, and even people's differences. Diversity broke out intermittently throughout the Church's history but an *overemphasis* on unity seemed to dominate much of its thinking. Then Vatican II brought us in balance once again. The classical unchanging worldview continued to be accepted, but there was now a need to yield to pluralism.

Adult religious education is experiencing the same milieu. With the richness of prayer forms, liturgical rites, and methods of small group learning, we are at an important crossroads when the creative energy of diversity can either be depleted or moved into a Spirit-filled Pentecost.

I am reminded of Perry's Intellectual and Ethical Line of Development (cf. *Effective Teaching and Mentoring* by Laurant A. Daloz, Jossey-Bass, Inc., Publishers, 1986, pp. 75-84.). This theory maintains that differentiation increases with maturity. Perhaps we are approaching differentiation (diversity) in our worldview—the culture is maturing as well. We are finally realizing the wisdom of adjusting to change, learning to prioritize, accepting (or at least tolerating) differences, incorporating complexity, knowing that black and white are not the only colors of the rainbow. With this slowly dawning realization, we are flexing the muscles of maturity.

Back to the Y . . . Fitness instructors tell us that no one exercise can get us totally fit. The same goes for adult education methods. There is time for centering techniques, mindmapping, brainstorming, praxis, lecture, panels, social analysis, dialogue groups, clarifying questions, journaling, force field analysis, audience participation, critical incidents, roleplaying, debate, etc. Each of these techniques, placed appropriately in learning situations, can help create a healthy tension between diversity and unity.

Tension is probably a good word to remember. There is always the push and pull, the reflex muscles of care and daring, the give and take of exploration and silence, the extension of unity by the reaching hand of diversity.

My last observation at the Y . . . Unity was maintained in all kinds of ways even though diversity was simultaneously happening. People seemed to care about the unifying values of limiting stress, enriching health, and caring for others around them. Most people I met there seemed genuinely concerned and helpful. They may be ruggedly competitive or happily contented with *beating* themselves. These are signs of unity even though they are the fruit of varied cultures, styles of living, and exercise habits.

I see the same thing in my adult education classes. People are maintaining their values thoughtfully even though they may need clarification or reflection. As a facilitator, I can't give them perseverance or joy. But I can work with their varied approaches to life and challenge them to act on their beliefs. I can yield to their diversity and stretch it until it, in turn, yields a unity of values and faith. It doesn't take force or reminders; it takes discovery, wonder, and loving dialogue.

The Social and Cultural Context of Adult Religious Education

Maurice L. Monette, OMI

Introduction

The social and cultural context is the *midst* or setting in which adult religious education takes place. As the terms indicate, that setting is composed of social structures (like churches, government, schools, businesses, families) and cultural meanings and patterns (that is, values or *ways of doing things* like democracy, individualism, or freedom).

The study and practice of adult religious education is not known for its attention to the social and cultural context. Yet such attention is sorely warranted on several counts:

(1) One of the goals of adult education is to "prepare believers to exercise a prophetic voice in today's world, to focus the light of the Gospel on the issues of our time" (*Catechesi Tradendae*, 43). Through pastoral letters, the bishops have challenged educators to respond to a specific social and cultural agenda.

(2) The teaching and planning of every educator is implicitly or explicitly informed by certain assumptions about the social and cultural context. Those assumptions are reflected for better or for worse in every educational function: goal setting, need assessment, the choice of content and process, and evaluation.

The challenge before adult educators is to make explicit the social and cultural analysis that informs educational planning and teaching and to engage adult Christians in their own analysis of key issues and concerns. Three questions need to be answered if we are to meet that challenge:

• What is social and cultural analysis?
• How does social and cultural analysis inform educational planning and teaching?
• What are some of the key characteristics of the social and cultural context of adult religious education in the U.S.?

I. What Is Social and Cultural Analysis?

The analysis of the social and cultural context (contextual analysis) is an attempt to make explicit and critically reflect upon one's assumptions about the milieu of ministry, so as to better discern within it the *signs of the times*, that is, the activity of God among us. Such analysis is more diagnostic than prescriptive. Its immediate purpose is not to yield solutions but to isolate the most important determining factors in a situation and to show causes, connections, and active forces. This analysis assures that assumptions are brought to full consciousness, tested for validity, critically examined, and exposed to the light of the Gospel.

Social analysis (or the contextual analysis of which we speak) is one component within *the pastoral circle*, a process of reflection and action which underlies all types of pastoral planning, including educational planning. The pastoral circle made familiar by Holland and Henriot includes four components, all of which accompany effective educational planning and teaching:

(1) Insertion. Telling our own stories of how social structures touch our lives and also meeting people who are suffering and abandoned at the edges of these structures.

(2) Social Analysis. Going beyond our stories and the issues involved and seeking the causes, actors, linkages, and consequences involved.

(3) Theological Reflection. Examining our situations in the light of the Gospel and the social teachings of the Church, thereby raising new questions, insights, and possible responses.

(4) Pastoral Planning. Choosing strategic action responses appropriate to our situations.[1]

These action responses in turn lead to new experiences. The pastoral circle begins anew, spiraling more deeply, more broadly, and all the while remaining open-ended.

The U.S. bishops have engaged in such analysis and have set the social agenda of the Church in the United States with their pastoral letters on racism, life issues (such as abortion), peace, and the economy. They have done so at great depth through consultation with experts from a variety of perspectives. They now propose their views for critical consideration by Catholics and other citizens. Local bishops and diocesan agencies have issued their own statements about issues which impact locally (e.g., the Appalachian pastoral, *This Land Is Home to Me*). Some local churches are resourced by centers of justice and peace and other organizations focused on particular issues. These have also issued statements, research, and educational aids.

But, adult educators also need to be social analysts inasmuch as

[1]Peter Henriot and Joe Holland, *Social Analysis* (New York: Orbis Books and Center of Concern, 1983), pp. 7–30.

their ministry takes place within a local context with its own particular issues and concerns.

The need for social and cultural analysis becomes most acute

(1) during a time of social crisis, as when segregation threatens an educational system or when drug abuse is locally becoming a serious problem or, as the bishops stated in their pastoral on peace, when the world is, as it is at present, at a "moment of supreme crisis,"

(2) when the parish or diocese or educational ministry is beginning a planning cycle, as when a new leader takes office or when a ministry is initiated or reorganized.

Whatever the circumstances, social and cultural analysis is a necessary ingredient in the process of realigning the Church (at every level of mission or ministry) to the reign of God as that reign is breaking into a particular social context.

Ideally, social and cultural analysis becomes for the pastoral minister a habit of the mind, a faculty operative each time the minister opens either the Bible or the newspaper.

II. How Does Social and Cultural Analysis Inform Educational Planning and Teaching?

Analysis of the social and cultural context is a critical tool for the fulfillment of the most crucial tasks of the educational policymaker, administrator, and facilitator: goal setting, the assessment of need, and the choice of appropriate process and content, and evaluation.[2] Solid notions about what kind of education is to be done and how it should be done derive in great part from accurate analysis of the social milieu.[3]

---

[2]The work of adult educators can be understood in terms of three roles: the policymaker, the administrator, and the facilitator. The policymaker is concerned with the overall direction of the organization and of the task of educating adults; the administrator manages a total program or set of courses; and the facilitator organizes and teaches a particular course. All their roles involve the tasks of goal setting, evaluation, need assessment, and choosing process and content—but on different organizational levels. These tasks are not necessarily completed in the order described. Evaluation often occurs, for instance, at the end of a particular course; but, as an administrative level task, it might also occur at the beginning of a new administrator's tenure.

[3]The sociocultural is only one of three sets of questions fundamental to the educational process. The other two are the psychological and the transactional, which deal with models of personhood and notions of the educational relationship. For a development of these three foundational categories, see James B. MacDonald and others, *Reschooling Society* (Alexandria, Virginia: The Association for Supervision and Curriculum Development, 1973).

A. Goal-Setting

The quality of the direction given to adult religious education at any one moment in history depends heavily on how astutely the Church's educators select which social forces they are to maximize or perpetuate.

The U.S. bishops have proposed that the Church maximize and perpetuate at least the following four social forces: the quest for peace in the world, racial equality, economic justice especially toward the poor, and respect for life from cradle to grave. Underlying this choice of options are the basic Christian values of human dignity, human development, and human rights.

The social agenda is clear: racism, abortion and other life issues, peace, and the economy. The analyses are on paper: *Brothers and Sisters To Us, The Challenge of Peace: God's Promise and Our Response, Economic Justice for All: Pastoral Letter on Catholic Social Teaching and the U.S. Economy.* The direction is set for educators to disseminate the teachings, pursue the analysis, and widen the dialogue.

Therefore, some of the analysis needed by adult educators is already available. But the work is not done. Two other tasks remain:

(1) the adaptation of the available analysis to local social realities,
(2) the application of the analysis to the planning and teaching of the practitioner.

The first task consists of
(1) critically reflecting on the analysis proposed by the bishops and others,
(2) making explicit and critiquing the adult educator's own assumptions about the social context,
(3) surfacing other issues which are particular to the local context of ministry.

The second task consists of applying the results of the analysis to the other educational functions named above: they are goal-setting, the assessment of need, the choice of appropriate process and content, and evaluation.

B. Need Assessment

Need assessment is a value laden and no mere fact-finding process. The easy part is the identification of the participants' *felt needs* or choice of programs. The hard part is deciding what programs to provide when the educator's perception of what the participants need differs from that of the participants. Since the 1970s *Me Decade*, prospective participants have mostly requested personal growth programs. Offerings related to current social problems have mostly met with rejection. Yet adult educators know that action on behalf of justice is central to the Christian faith and that they have been commissioned by the Church to teach in that area. How is the educator to fulfill that responsibility when the participants do not identify that area as a *felt need*?

The educator's choice of response in such a situation avoids either mere acquiescence to felt needs or sheer imposition of authority. The provision of requested programs relating to personal growth can be coupled with a choice of content and process which in some way addresses the *causes* or origins of the felt need for personal growth. Paulo Freire pursues such an approach to literacy education in Brazil, and Robert Bellah does so for the U.S. context in his analysis of individualism.[4] At least one recently published education and retreat program pursues Christian social responsibility through a discussion of personal growth and conversion experiences.[5] The most effective approaches to the social dimension of faith begin where people are in their own development and challenges them to see their development as tied to that of society.

C. Content and Process

The choice of content and process is based, as is every other major curriculum decision, on assumptions about the social context. The social agenda proposed by the bishops would suggest that adult religious education content and process include the following.

(1) Skill training for
- critical reflection, so that the faithful can contribute to the discussion of social issues such as those raised in the pastoral letters;
- consultation, a skill which leaders need in order to listen to the experience of the faithful;
- social analysis coupled with theological analysis, in order to reflect on social realities from the perspective of the Gospel;
- peacemaking skills such as conflict resolution, crisis management, and listening.

(2) Educational approaches and instruction that are based on theologies and spiritualities which have social, personal, and interpersonal dimensions. These dimensions would be, for example,

[4]Paulo Freire, *Pedagogy of the Oppressed* (New York: The Seabury Press, 1970); Robert N. Bellah and others, *Habits of the Heart: Individualism and Commitment in American Life* (Berkeley: University of California Press, 1985).
[5]Maurice L. Monette, *The Supper Table: Programs for Community Spirituality* (Kansas City, Missouri: Sheed and Ward, 1985).

creation-centered, sensitive to the needs of the poor and of the Third World, based on the social texts of the Gospels, baptismal and mission-centered, and lay-centered (inclusive of the experiences of work, family, sexuality, marketplace, and leisure).

(3) Curricula that includes the *pastoral circle* approach as well as social analysis methods.

(4) The use of curriculum resources such as those produced by the major Catholic publishers and by organizations like the American Catholic Lay Network, the Center of Concern, Global Associates, LEAVEN, the Institute for the Study of Peace and Justice, Network, the Quixote Center, and the U. S. Catholic Conference.

This list is not intended to be inclusive, just suggestive of the implications that a social agenda can have for adult religious education curriculum.

D. *Evaluation*

The directions chosen for adult education are based upon prescriptive as well as evaluative criteria. In other words, they suggest what adult education should look like as well as how it should be evaluated. Our discussion so far suggests the following criteria:

Effective adult religious education
(1) selects goals that are consistent with the social agenda proposed by the bishops,
(2) challenges participants' felt needs when these overlook the social and cultural dimension of faith,
(3) proposes theological and spiritual content that is consistent with the Church's social agenda,
(4) teaches skills and utilizes educational methods that promote the social agenda of the Church.

In summary, social and cultural analysis provides the adult religious educator with
(1) rationales for socially-realistic educational goal-setting,
(2) better understanding of the causes or origins of the expressed needs of the participants,
(3) suggestions about appropriate content and processes,
(4) criteria for evaluating education efforts.

III. What Are Some of the Key Characteristics of the Social and Cultural Context of Adult Religious Education in the U.S.?

As we adult educators seriously engage in social and cultural analysis, any number of key characteristics will grasp our attention, depending of course on regional, ethnic, historical, and other background differences. At this time, however, informed by but the slimmest of research, we can clearly recognize a few key contextual characteristics that affect our educational planning and teaching. The following list is not complete. It is only one attempt to identify some of the social and cultural variables which call for our attention.

A. Democracy

The several polls taken before the recent visit to the U.S. by Pope John Paul II indicate that U.S. Catholics strongly desire a say in the ecclesial decisions that affect their lives. They want their experience to matter in Church decisions about the morality of birth control, abortion, and sexual orientation; they want a say in how their Sunday collections are spent; and they want to participate in the ministries of the Church. This democratic sense of participation is deep in the psyche of a Catholicism that survived a priestless frontier, elected a bishop, and administered parishes through lay trustees. Americans love their parish and do not easily abandon their responsibility for its growth and survival.

B. Pluralism

Catholicism in the United States has learned to live with pluralism, both internally and externally. It includes practically anyone who is willing to tolerate the differences existing among its members. It exists side by side with Protestant denominations, with other religions, and with social groups holding widely divergent views. But Catholicism in the U.S. also suffers from the concommitant lack of moral consensus and forums for moral deliberation through which widely divergent views can be reconciled in search for truth. This is the problem addressed by Robert Bellah and others in *Habits of the Heart*.

C. The Women's Movement

The powerful demand for the recognition of the dignity and rights of women is, perhaps, unequaled in any other society in the world. Little wonder the world Catholic Church is not quick to respond to the challenge of the American Catholic women calling for changes in church discipline and attitudes.

D. Wealth and Global Influence

What does it mean to be Catholic in a materialistic country when two-thirds of the world and the majority of world Catholics live in poverty? The bishops' pastorals on the economy and on peace address a constellation of such issues.

E. The Growing Complexity of Family Life

The nuclear family with two parents and children can no longer be presumed in pastoral practice. Single-parent households, childless couples, and reconstituted families are some of the many forms that family life takes today. Also, increasing numbers of Catholics are exercising their own consciences on such matters as divorce, birth control, and abortion. How to deal with these issues as well as those regarding the proper care of children and the strengthening of the family poses challenges for both Church and society.

These and other key characteristics of American culture and society cannot escape the attention of the effective adult religious educator engaged in the planning and teaching functions of need assessment, goal setting, choice of content and process, and evaluation. Ignorance of the milieu condemns education to irrelevance and ineffectiveness.

Conclusion

Adult educators might select as their own that goal which C. Wright Mills proposed for social scientists, namely, the development of *sociological imagination*. He defines it as a

> quality of mind that helps us use information and develop reason in order to achieve lucid summations of what is going on in the world and what may be happening within ourselves.[6]

From the Christian perspective that quality of sociological imagination would include the abilities to

(1) identify what is going on in the world and within ourselves in the light of the Gospel,
(2) remember the social dimensions of the biblical story and of the Church's own journey through history,
(3) identify what our society and culture should and could be in the light of the Christian vision,
(4) commit ourselves and our communities to take action on behalf of justice and peace.

The ability to arrive at lucid summations of what is and should be happening in the world counteracts the contemporary tendencies to succumb to powerlessness, reactionary fear, or apathy. It is a goal consistent with a social agenda like ours which seeks to respect human dignity, foster human development, and promote human rights.

---

[6]C. Wright Mills, *The Sociological Imagination* (New York: Grove Press, Inc., 1959), p. 5.

The Challenge to Be Relevant and Effective: A Response to The Social and Cultural Content of Adult Religious Education

Matthew Hayes

After reading and reflecting upon Maurice's article, and aware of my task to draw out some practical implications, I am continually haunted by his comment: "Ignorance of the milieu condemns education to irrelevance and ineffectiveness." What is more practical for adult educators than striving to be relevant and effective? How often have I found my adult religious education efforts (at both the parish and diocesan levels) to be ineffective, sometimes irrelevant, and, therefore, of poor practice!

I will offer my reflections on practical implications in three areas: the vision of the adult religious educator, the method of program planning, and the practice of adult religious education. In addition, I will close with some further questions that Maurice's thoughts have sparked.

Implications for Vision

The vision area concerns the scope of adult religious education. As Maurice has written: "The study and practice of adult religious education is not known for its attention to the social and cultural context." I feel one of the reasons for this neglect is the view that limits the scope of adult religious education is not known for its attention to the *social and cultural context*. I feel one of the reasons for this neglect is the view that limits the scope of adult religious education to explicitly religious content. Social and cultural analysis, as described by Maurice, calls for a scope that is wide-open. In the 1983 edition of *Christian Adulthood*, Leon McKenzie clearly made the case for an open-ended scope.[1] Without an open scope, the adult educator, as program planner, cannot *fully* invite parishioners into the first movement of the pastoral circle. Contrary to what we might hope, the lives of most Catholics are not deeply influenced by religious social structures that

[1]Leon McKenzie, "Foundations: The Scope, Purposes and Goals of Adult Religious Education," in *Christian Adulthood: A Catechetical Resource, 1983* (Washington, D.C.: USCC Office of Publishing and Promotion Services, 1983) pp. 17–20.

touch their lives. Rather, they are impacted by economic, work-related, and family-focused issues.

I have found the thinking of Jurgen Habermas to be very helpful as I try to clarify the scope of adult religious education. His three types of knowledge (above the broken lines in the adjacent figure) are parallel to a balanced approach to catechesis (below the broken lines in the adjacent figure) as presented in the documents *To Teach As Jesus Did*, and *Sharing the Light of Faith*.[2] Such a scope, particularly in the area of emancipatory knowledge, opens up the scope of adult religious education to the social analysis for which Maurice is calling.

Implications for Program Planning

As Maurice has indicated, the process of reflection and action contained in the *pastoral circle* not only accompanies effective educational planning, but can actually become an alternative method for program planning. Typically, the adult religious educator follows a program planning model which includes needs assessment, objective formulation, delivery of learning, and evaluation. In his article (and elsewhere[3]), Maurice pointed out that the needs assessment process has an active dimension. The adult religious educator can consciously develop programs as one of the strategic actions in the fourth component of the pastoral circle. This takes all the benefits of program planning based on participants' felt needs and couples it with the benefits of an approach based on institutional needs. If done effectively, the potential adult religious education participant will be motivated to become involved because the program is tied to *the stories* of how social structures touch his/her life. Such a method calls for the adult educator (and not only the participants in a program) to develop skills in consultation and critical reflection.

Another implication for program planning methods in adult religious education is for the adult educator no longer to treat the parish as a whole. Rather, he/she should target program planning efforts

---

[2]National Conference of Catholic Bishops, *To Teach as Jesus Did: A Pastoral Message on Catholic Education* (Washington, D.C.: USCC Office of Publishing and Promotion Services, 1973); USCC Department of Education, *Sharing the Light of Faith: National Catechetical Directory for Catholics of the United States* (Washington, D.C.: USCC Office of Publishing and Promotion Services, 1979).

[3]Maurice Monette, "Educational Planning: Responding Responsibly," in *Christian Adulthood: A Catechetical Resource, 1982* (Washington, D.C.: USCC Office of Publishing and Promotion Services, 1982) pp. 17–20.

Three Kinds of Knowledge
The Scope of Adult Religious Education

KNOWLEDGE	FOCUS	OUTCOME	PROCESS
Technical knowledge.	Information, Ideas, and Concepts.	Mastery of information generated by researchers and theoreticians.	Analysis and application of ideas.
Message Information.	*Scripture, Doctrines, Teachings.*	*To understand and own the tradition.*	*Reflection upon the meaning of the tradition.*
Practical knowledge.	Human interactions in a group/ community.	Change in lifestyle orientation. Affective change.	Formal Level: Interpretive analysis of human interactions. Informal Level: Unconscious assilimation of *spirit* and values of the group/ community.
Community Formation.	*Building of relationships.*	*Support and challenge in living values of the tradition.*	*Faith sharing.*
Emancipatory Knowledge.	The manifest and hidden assumptions that limit creativity, growth, and behavior.	Bringing to light and critique of hidden assumptions. Identification and critique of manifest assumptions.	Critical self-reflection.
Service Transformation.	*Areas of personal and societal need.*	*A fuller life.*	*Reflection/action.*

Chart adapted from Jurgen Habermas' *Knowledge and Human Interests* (Boston: Beacon Press, 1971).

upon specific segments of the parish that are influenced by similar social structures.[4]

Cultural and social issues of one's life appear in the concrete, in the *hot issues* that one feels. As the adult educator inserts and immerses

---

[4]For a specific approach to needs assessment based upon segments, see my article: "A

himself/herself into the context of the learner, critically reflects upon it to become aware of *causes, action, linkages, and consequences involved,* and examines it in the light of the Catholic tradition, action strategies (adult religious programs that address these hot issues) emerge. So, the task of social analysis, as part of the pastoral circle, can become an alternative method of program design.

Implications for Practice

An implication of taking seriously the social and cultural context of the learner is to consciously and consistently address his/her role as a worker and as citizen.

The learner as worker is becoming more prominent in adult religious education. Some examples are the work of Robert Reber[5] at Auburn and the consultation on work and faith that took place at Notre Dame in October 1983.[6] In addition, Fortress Press has two resources designed for six-week discussion groups that deal with the connection between work and faith: *All In A Day's Work: Ministry on the Job,* and *Monday's Ministries.*

The adult as worker can also be addressed by targeting a particular segment of the parish that shares a similar profession or a similar place of employment. For example, I participated in a Lenten lunchtime lecture discussion series at the corporate headquarters of Eli Lilly and Company in downtown Indianapolis.

The adult as citizen, as Maurice has pointed out, is emphasized in recent pastorals of the U.S. bishops. In the last few years, I have encouraged parish adult education committees to engage parishioners as citizens by using resources such as the National Issues Forum (NIF) material, sponsored by the Domestic Policy Association of the Kettering Foundation. NIF is a nationwide, nonpartisan program of public issue discussion which does not advocate any specific solution or point of view on public issues but seeks to provide a means by which citizens can gain an influential role in public policy making. Each year, the NIF identifies three issues for public discussion in the fall/winter. Attractive, well-written, participant booklets are prepared for each issue, along with broadcast quality videotapes. Locally-sponsored gatherings (forums) take place in which citizens reflect on the choices that face them in addressing the issues. The opinions of those who

Different Approach to Needs Assessment," in *Christian Adulthood: A Catechetical Resource, 1987* (Washington, D.C.: USCC Office of Publishing and Promotion Services, 1987), pp. 35–39.
[5]Robert Reber, "Vocation and Vision: A New Look at the Mission of the Laity," *Auburn News,* Fall 1987, pp. 1–8.
[6]Maurice Monette, *Work and Faith in Society: A Handbook for Dioceses and Parishes* (Washington, D.C.: United States Catholic Conference, 1986).

participated in the forum are registered through a national summary prepared by the Domestic Policy Association. The summary is later used by representative forum participants to address local, state, and national legislators in the spring.

I have found that the NIF process is good for helping parishioners reflect on the social justice tradition of the Church by consciously considering the Church's response to the issue (after the issue has been fully considered from the perspective of the NIF materials).[7]

A curriculum resource from Fortress Press, *Neighbor Talk: Community Issues* which outlines a six-session series for discussion about (and influence upon) community change around concerns identified by the participants and a *Discussion Guide for Addressing Community and Social Issues* published by the Division of Parish Services of the Lutheran Church of America are two resources that directly enable participants in adult religious education to reflect upon the social and cultural context.[8]

Further Questions

As a practitioner of adult religious education, there are a few questions that Maurice's thoughts have sparked. How are the roles described in *Ministering to the Adult Learner: A Skills Workbook for Christian Educational Leaders* (as program planner, as teacher/facilitator, and as administrator) parallel to his three *crucial tasks* (educational policymaker, administrator, and facilitator)?[9] I feel the field of adult religious education would be better served if we could reflect on how social and cultural analysis is a critical tool for fulfilling each of these roles. In addition, I would have liked Maurice to describe how *each* of his *crucial tasks* (or each of the three roles) are impacted in the areas of goal setting, needs assessment, content and process, and evaluation. Such a description would have enabled the reader to discern more carefully the relevance of social and cultural analysis to his/her tasks (or roles).

I am appreciative of Maurice's description of some of the key characteristics of United States culture that impact adult religious education. Adult religious educators need to expand and refine his list. In addition, we need to articulate how these characteristics enable or

---

[7]For additional information about the National Issues Forum, write: National Issues Forum, 100 Commons Road, Dayton, Ohio, 45459-2777.

[8]The *Discussion Guide for Community and Social Issues* can be obtained from: The Division for Parish Services, Lutheran Church in America, 2900 Queen Lane, Philadelphia, Pennsylvania, 19129.

[9]Jane Wolford Hughes, Editor, *Ministering to Adult Learners: A Skills Workbook for Christian Educational Leaders* (Washington, D.C.: USCC Office of Publishing and Promition Services, 1981).

hinder our efforts. For example, what are the implications that flow from the democratic sense of participation that is so deep within our culture as we attempt to work as adult educators in an authoritarian tradition?[10] How does pluralism enhance adult religious education efforts that value learners themselves as resources? How does the disintegration of the nuclear family impact the learner who brings, and returns to, a communal context that enhances or hinders the learning process?

These further questions are simply offered in an atmosphere of respect and appreciation: respect for the insights Maurice brings and appreciation for the contributions he is making to enable adult religious education to become more effective and relevant.

[10]For a consideration of this issue, see James Schaefer's article, "Tensions between Adult Growth and Church Authority" in *Christian Adulthood: A Catechetical Resource, 1982* (Washington, D.C.: USCC Office of Publishing and Promotion Services, 1982), pp. 21–32.

Loretta Girzaitis is coordinator of Adult Education for the Archdiocese of St. Paul/Minneapolis; St. Paul, Minnesota.

Fred Eyerman is coordinator for Adult Education; Archdiocese of Denver, Colorado.

David M. Thomas, Ph.D., is director of the graduate program in Adult Christian Community Development; Regis College; Denver, Colorado.

Jane Wolford Hughes is a consultant in adult religious education and former director of Adult Education, Archdiocese of Detroit.

John L. Elias, Ph.D., is the director of Programs in Adult Religious Education and Development; Graduate School of Religion and Religious Education; Fordham University; New York, New York.

John L. Zaums, Ph.D., is chair of the Religous Studies Department; Marywood College; Scranton, Pennsylvania.

C. Michael Lebrato is executive secretary, National Conference of Diocesan Directors of Religious Education—CCD; Washington, D.C.

Alice M. Stefaniak is director of Adult Religious Education; Diocese of Jefferson City; Jefferson City, Missouri.

Maurice L. Monette, OMI, Ed.D., is a consultant and researcher in adult religious education and lay ministry.

Matthew Hayes is director of Religious Education/coordinator of Adult Catechesis; Archdiocese of Indianapolis; Indianapolis, Indiana.

DATE DUE